LIFT YOUR SAILS

LIFT YOUR SAILS

SAILS

*The Challenge of
Being a Christian*

Vincent Dwyer, OCSO

CONTINUUM • NEW YORK

1999

The Continuum Publishing Company
370 Lexington Avenue
New York, NY 10017

Printed in the United States of America

Second, Revised Edition

Library of Congress Cataloging-in-Publication Data

Dwyer, Vincent
    Lift your sails : the challenge of being a christian / Vincent Dwyer.
—2nd rev. ed.
        p.   cm.
    Includes bibliographical references.
    ISBN 0-8264-1139-8
    1. Spiritual life—Catholic Church.   I. Title
BX2350.2.D89   1999
248.4'82—dc21   98-52848
                                                                  CIP

Grateful acknowledgment is made to the following for permission to quote
from previously published material:
    Cistercian Publications for excerpts from Aelred of Rievaulx, *On Spiritual
Friendship,* translated by Mary Eugenia Laker, S.S.N.D., copyright © 1977 and
used with permission of the publisher.
    Doubleday & Company, Inc., for excerpts from *The Cloud of Unknowing,*
edited by William Johnston, an Image Books original, copyright © 1973 and
used with permission of the publisher.
    Harcourt Brace Jovanovich, Inc., for excerpts from *The Four Loves,* by C. S.
Lewis, copyright © 1960 by Helen Joy Lewis and used with permission of the
publisher.
    Jossey Bass Publishing, Inc., for excerpts from *Measuring Ego Development*
by J. Loevinger, J. Wessler, and C. Redmore, copyright © 1970 and used with
permission of the publisher.
    United States Catholic Conference for excerpts from the English translation
of *Ecclesiam Suam (Paths of the Church)* by Pope Paul VI, copyright © 1964; *The
Lord and Giver of Life* by Pope John Paul II, copyright © 1986; and *Sects or New
Religious Movements: Pastoral Challenge,* copyright © 1985. Used with permission of the publisher.

CONTENTS

PREFACE

A FEW YEARS after *Lift Your Sails* was first published in 1987, I was able to return to St. Joseph's Abbey in Spencer, Massachusetts, where I first became a monk over forty years ago. It was a pleasure to return to the monastic life. It almost seemed as though I had never been away.

A few years later, I was diagnosed with cancer, for which I've had to receive several rounds of chemotherapy. A little less than a year ago, my doctors decided I needed a period of rest, so I came to one of my community's daughter houses, St. Benedict's Monastery in Snowmass, Colorado. It has been a wonderful time for reflection and prayer, and I'm deeply grateful to the community for receiving me with an attitude of warmth, love, and care. Like many people who have been told they have cancer, I've found that the news brought me back to the fundamentals of the spiritual life. In this regard, cancer has been a great gift.

I had not read *Lift Your Sails* since it was published and worried that it might seem a little dated. However, in rereading it, I am gratified to find that it has remained relevant, that it still responds to the spiritual hunger of people today. The challenge of Christ was as clear as day when he told us to love one another as he loves us. Each of us faces, generation after generation, this same challenge. We must not give in to our fear of loving; we must not avoid love for fear of getting hurt. Rather, we must remain committed to seeking the freedom and joy that only true love and friendship can confer.

Lift Your Sails remains as relevant today as it was when it was first published because it responds to questions and concerns that we encounter on our journeys regardless of the time and place in which we find ourselves. It draws on what our spiritual tradition teaches us about love, friendship, woundedness, forgiveness, and prayer. And in doing so, it helps us to awaken to our true selves, created in the image and likeness of God.

Since my return to the monastic life, I have become increasingly convinced that the key to happiness, fulfillment, and achieving balance is a daily life of prayer. Prayer is the choice we make to place ourselves in the presence of God, and taking time to do so each morning and evening is absolutely essential. As we enter into the stillness and silence of prayer, we set aside all our thoughts, perceptions, and judgments, and open ourselves to experiencing his healing presence in our lives. As I look back on my own journey, I realize that whenever it felt as though I were drifting away from God, I had abandoned the daily practice of prayer. I urge you to begin and end each day by spending some time in his presence. You'll see a great change in how you respond to others and the events of the day.

You'll find a "Suggested Reading" section at the end of this book. It lists a number of works that I've found especially helpful on my journey. I believe the wisdom they contain transcends time and cultural shifts. You may also find them helpful on your own spiritual journey.

I am deeply grateful to everyone at Continuum, especially to Gene Gollogly, for encouraging me to bring *Lift Your Sails* back into print. I'd also like to express my thanks to Jake Holden, who helped me with the revisions for this edition. I couldn't have done it without his help.

May you lift your own sails, pull up the anchors, and let the Holy Spirit guide your course through the exciting adventure of life that leads to the Father. God bless you!

Snowmass, Colorado

INTRODUCTION

O NE OF THE greatest gifts I have received in this life is to have witnessed time and again the extraordinary power of forgiveness and love. There is no human experience that can compare to that of a soul who, through human understanding and reconciliation, begins to taste the cosmic and all-embracing love of God. This book is borne from my reflections on this miraculous love, and one of my chief goals in writing it has been to help unleash the reader's own potential for love, for forgiveness, and for growth.

The message of love and forgiveness is as old as Christianity itself. Indeed, it is older; it is timeless. But even eternal wine must be placed in new bottles due to the vicissitudes of time. We must continually find new ways to speak about these changeless realities and bring them to fruition. Like any perspective, mine is not perfect or complete. It is simply the vision I have been granted on my own journey. The reality of love is as expansive as the universe itself, reaching far beyond the boundaries of Christian dogma. It is the beating heart in all that lives, and all religions in one way or another address themselves to it. Nevertheless, I was raised in the Catholic Church, and its own particular vision has come to be the marrow of my being. When I speak of God's love I cannot but speak of the revelation of Jesus Christ. Therefore, this book will speak most clearly to those who have accepted the message of Christ and are trying to follow him.

Our times have witnessed the breakdown of traditional religious forms and their replacement by all sorts of partial and fragmentary ideologies. There is an aching hunger in the "streets" of our time—a hunger for meaning! As a Christian, I firmly believe that our spiritual heritage has a great deal to offer in facing our existential predicament. At the same time, there are a number of behavioral scientists in the front ranks of those who are trying to address the problem of human meaning, and their insights can be extremely helpful in shedding light on the meaning and richness of our Christian heritage. Today we find an enormous amount of literature dealing with human growth and development, and this body of knowledge can be a tremendous tool in understanding our journey to the Father, a journey that begins at birth and continues through death to the resurrection. This lifelong journey is often referred to as a process of education or formation. However we choose to describe it, we *must* recognize that it is of paramount importance. Education, as we all know, can take place in many ways, and since this is a book of words and thoughts, you'll find at the end a list of suggested readings which can help you to wade further into the stream.

From my early days I have asked a great many questions in search of meaning. I wanted to know how to live an exciting life—a life that would in some way make a difference. When I was very young, a very dear and holy person in my parish showed me *The Scale of Perfection,* by the fourteenth-century English mystic, Walter Hilton. I found it interesting but it seemed too simple, and some of its language had little meaning to my understanding of life. It now has great meaning as I grow older and I encourage you to reflect and pray on the following passage:

> There was a man who wanted to go to Jerusalem. And because he didn't know how to get there, he went to another man who, as he hoped, knew the way there. He asked this man how he could get to Jerusalem. The other man told him that he wouldn't be able to get there without great discomfort and much hard labor, for the road was long and perilous, full of thieves and robbers, and that there were many other obstacles which would befall the man on this journey.

Also, he explained, there were many different roads which seemed to lead to Jerusalem, but people traveling them were continually being killed and robbed and were unable to arrive at the place they desired. Nevertheless, he continued, there was one way which he could promise would lead anyone who would take it and stay with it, to the city of Jerusalem. Nor would such a man lose his life; he would neither be slain nor die by default. Although he would be robbed frequently, be cruelly beaten, and suffer much discomfort in his journeying, his life would always be safe.

Then the pilgrim answered, "As long as I'll keep my life safe and will come to the place I desire, I don't care what evils I suffer in the process. Therefore, tell me whatever you want, and truly, I must do what you say."

The other man answered, "Look, I'll point you in the right direction. This is the right road. And so that you can hold on to the instructions I am going to give you, pay no attention to anything you hear, see, or experience that would divert you from this path. Don't deliberately stay with such things; don't delight in them, nor waste your time relaxing in them; don't even look at them. Instead, always keep moving ahead on your journey. Think always that you want to be at Jerusalem, for it is Jerusalem you covet, Jerusalem you desire, and nothing else but Jerusalem.

"Now if men rob you and take what you have, if they beat you, throw stones at you, despise you, don't fight back if you want to hold on to your life. Be content with the harm you have suffered and go on as if it were nothing, so that you may not receive any further harm.

"Again, if men want to delay you with stories and feed you with lies in order to draw you into amusements and cause you to abandon your pilgrimage, turn a deaf ear and don't respond to them. Say nothing except that you want to be at Jerusalem. Further, if men offer you gifts and want to make you rich with worldly goods, pay no attention to them. Just concentrate always on Jerusalem.

"If you stick to this road and do as I have said, I promise you your life; you won't be slain, and you will come to the place you desire."[1]

---

1. Walter Hilton, *The Scale of Perfection,* trans. Dom Gerard Sitwell, L.S.B. (London: Burns and Oates, 1953), 192–93.

When we respond to Christ's invitation to follow him, we set out on a journey. Our journey is filled with mystery—pain, suffering, misunderstandings, hurts, disappointments, joys, successes, and, at times, happiness and a sense of fulfillment. These words describe the ups and downs, the peaks of the mountains and also the valleys; they describe life—our own personal journey. This journey is not meant to be boring or routine—it is a spiritual adventure. For God *is* life! He reveals himself through people, the church, events—he can be found in everyday life. The struggle of the spiritual life is the challenge to respond to his revelation, a revelation that takes place from moment to moment. Spirituality is then the integrating focus for all aspects of growth and change. Your unique response to God revealing himself on your journey is what it's all about. Your journey is not an isolated part of your life; it involves your whole being spiritually, emotionally, physically, and intellectually. It is a lifelong process that requires your personal commitment to the process of growth which will require change and conversion in reaching the fullness of your gifts and talents—in knowing and tasting not only your own unique beauty but also the love of God!

Catholic tradition holds that each of us is blessed with certain gifts and talents whose fullness we are called to realize and experience in the course of our lives. Unfortunately, we often set up obstacles, either consciously or unconsciously, and set limits on these gifts, and on ourselves. Too often, we lose sight of our call to real fulfillment, and focus instead on merely surviving. As a result, it becomes necessary to deal with such fundamental issues as self-image and the realization of our gifts before we can arrive at a deeper level of spirituality. While the heart of spirituality is deeply rooted in the gospel, the manner in which each of us lives out the gospel is within the context of our own particular time and culture. Karl Rahner writes that "truly realized Christianity is always the achieved synthesis on each occasion of the message of the gospel and the grace of Christ, on the one hand, and the concrete situation in which the gospel is to be lived on the other."[2]

* * *

In 1955 I entered St. Joseph's Abbey in Spencer, Massachusetts, believing that I would spend the rest of my life living the simple life of a Trappist monk. Leaving the world of my family, friends, and work was quite difficult, but I was convinced that God had called me to the monastic life. Before I entered the monastery, I had searched for God in a number of different places. Several times, I thought I had found him, only to realize that my feet were not on the path that he was calling me to walk with him. Fortunately, he never gave up on me, so on that great day when I made my solemn vows before my monastic community I thought that I had arrived! Life would now be stable, secure, full of meaning, and I would be supported on my journey by men who had made the same commitment as me. But in the late sixties, I became ill and it was determined that my medical problems made it impossible for me to continue living the strict Trappist life. Under the advice of my doctor, the abbot decided that I should take a medical leave of absence from the community and pursue a doctorate in sacred theology at Catholic University.

My whole world seemed to be falling apart. I remember so well the feelings that came over me when I was told of the decision. I looked out my window in Massachusetts General Hospital in Boston and my heart cried out, "Why?" The road that led to the monastery had been one of ups and downs—an incredible struggle between God and my own desires. I had entered the seminary twice and left twice, convinced that it wasn't my call. I wanted more than anything to be married and have a family, but each time I set out to achieve this goal I found myself being pulled from within. So, when I entered the

---

2. Karl Rahner, *Theological Investigations*, vol. 5 (Baltimore: Helicon Press, 1960), 139.

monastery, I believed that I had finally given all I had to God. And over the years I had grown to love the way of life and the community in which I lived.

Suddenly, I was being asked to let go and follow him in a new way. Needless to say, I felt lonely and afraid; the future was completely uncertain to me. It was indeed one of the most difficult moments of my journey. And yet, as I now look back, I know that it was a major turning point in my life. For although I felt abandoned by God and suffered the terrible feeling of having lost all that I had come to cherish so deeply, I know now that he was guiding me every step of the way. The transition from monastic life to the academic world was most challenging. And the hardest thing he was asking of me was to let go of my old and familiar way of following him, and begin anew to listen to him in and through the unfolding events of my journey, endeavoring continually to respond to whatever he wanted of me.

During my years at Catholic University I began to feel more deeply than ever that there was a tremendous hunger to discover the rich heritage of the church. In the midst of not only a changing world but also a changing church, many Catholics seemed lost and confused and were searching for some way to make sense of their lives. I deeply believed that the insights of the saints and the great men and women who had gone before us had a great deal to offer in this regard. Vatican II was a tremendous challenge to all of us: priests, religious, and laity. Each of us was faced with the necessity of conversion, of shifting our view points on many things that had become part of us. Like myself, perhaps you too felt that, in a world that was constantly changing, at least the church would remain as it had always been—it was the one area of our lives that seemed stable and secure. Suddenly, it seemed that out of nowhere the very church that had given us so much security, that had handed down the rules that enabled us to fulfill our duties and obligations as Catholics was challenging us to let go and once again become pilgrims on a journey.

During this intense period of change in the church, priests, religious, and laity participated in all kinds of programs which were geared toward updating the church and assisting Catholics in making the transition from the old to the new. Initially, these programs for renewal focused on important shifts in the church's perspectives on theology, scripture, philosophy, and the hard sciences. Unfortunately, in many instances they failed to build bridges, becoming instead sources of tension, frustration, and even division. Even today, many of us are still struggling to meet the challenges of Vatican II. Meanwhile, the urgency of helping people to achieve a meaningful synthesis of their spiritual roots with the concrete situation of their lives has never been greater.

Those of us who grew up in the pre-Vatican II church can easily recall the difficulties that we encountered as the church began to implement changes. Sadly, many of these changes were concerned with altering forms of worship which had become for many Catholics a way of life. Turning the altar to face the people and eliminating certain devotions and practices left a good many of us feeling lost. Even more unfortunate was the fact that this focus on externals was not doing nearly enough to bring about the conversion of heart, the renewal of faith and the spiritual life which were the true goals of Vatican II. As I made the transition from the monastic to the academic life, I became convinced that the real challenge facing the church was to help Catholics *fully and authentically internalize* the Good News of Jesus Christ. The message of the gospel and the true principles of the Christian life had to be at the *very heart* of renewal, and I felt certain that helping people to internalize these truths was one of the most important tasks facing the church in our day.

*   *   *

After completing my doctorate I became a professor at the University of North Carolina at Charlotte. During my three years there I began to look for ways to create a vehicle that would respond to the spiritual hunger that I had encountered everywhere I went, and help Catholics to make the message of the gospel truly their own. I finally founded the Center for Human Development in 1972 as such a vehicle, to minister to the interior needs of priests, religious, and laity. The center's mission was to surface the teachings of Christ and the great spiritual masters so that people in our time could see that Christ is the way, and that in him is the true meaning of our journey; that only by turning to Christ and responding to his invitation to follow him could we hope to change ourselves, the church, and the world. I believed people wanted to grow, that they wanted to know Christ, and above all, that they wanted to learn the art of friendship and love. The Good News of the Christ event is incredible—it is, as I so often say, too good to be true, but true! I wanted the world to know that the meaning of life is found in him, and that to say "yes" to his invitation to follow him is to set out on an exciting adventure—a great love affair!

The Center for Human Development was first established at St. Mary's College in Winona, Minnesota. The center then moved to the University of Notre Dame in 1975 and finally, in 1980, it again moved to Washington, D.C. Each of these moves was spurred by the expansion of programs as well as a need for additional resources and greater interaction with other national and international organizations serving the church. Through research and the development of workshops, lectures, and retreats, the center seeks to communicate the Good News of our Christian heritage to today's church in ways that give it greater meaning, vision, and hope. It promotes holistic spiritual growth by integrating insights from the Christian tradition, the behavioral sciences, and our own personal experiences. And it collaborates with a network of institutions and research centers throughout the world to promote, foster, and assist the renewal of the church—THE PEOPLE OF GOD.

The CHD's Ministry to Priests Program has touched the lives of over forty thousand priests in over one hundred archdioceses and dioceses throughout the English speaking world. More than twenty religious orders of men and women have embraced our Ministry to Religious Program. The center also designed a program ministering to the chaplains of the United States military services, and assists seminaries and formation groups in developing programs to respond to their particular needs.

In 1975 I developed Genesis II, which was the first multimedia program designed to assist the laity in spiritual renewal. This program over the years has touched the lives of millions of people. The center went on to develop Pathways–Journeys in Spiritual Growth, which embraces a number of individual multimedia programs being used by many to foster growth and community.

These and other programs have enabled the center to touch the lives of a great many people over the past fifteen years. As I look back over these years, and the terrific work the center has been able to accomplish, I am filled with gratitude to God for all of his blessings. The contributions of the many outstanding individuals who have worked with me over the years have enabled the center to continue to develop better ways of serving people.

The challenge that the center attempted to respond to when it was founded in 1972 is, in my estimation, even more acute today, fifteen years later. On May 22, 1986, the Vatican issued a document, "Vatican Report on Sects, Cults and New Religious Movements," which emphasizes the urgency that we face in effectively communicating the rich spiritual heritage that *does* respond to the problems people face in their daily lives. The document places before us under four major headings what most of us are experiencing in family, church, and society:

1. QUEST FOR BELONGING

The fabric of many communities has been destroyed; traditional lifestyles have been disrupted; homes are broken up; people feel uprooted and lonely. Thus the need to belong. Terms used in the responses: belonging, love, community, communication, warmth, concern, care, support, friendship, affection, fraternity, help, solidarity, encounter, dialogue, consolation, acceptance, understanding, sharing, closeness, mutuality, togetherness, fellowship, reconciliation, tolerance, roots, security, refuge, protection, safety, shelter, home.

2. SEARCH FOR WHOLENESS

Many people feel that they are out of touch with themselves, with others, with their culture and environment. They experience brokenness. They have been hurt by parents or teachers, by the church or society. They feel left out. They want a religious view that can harmonize everything and everybody; worship which leaves room for body and soul, for participation, spontaneity, creativity.

3. NEED TO BE RECOGNIZED, TO BE SPECIAL

People feel a need to rise out of anonymity, to build an identity, to feel that they are in some way special and not just a number or a faceless member of a crowd. Large parishes and congregations, administration-oriented concern and clericalism, leave little room for approaching every person individually and in the person's life situation.

4. SEARCH FOR TRANSCENDENCE

This expresses a deeply spiritual need, a God-inspired motivation to seek something beyond the obvious, the immediate, the familiar, the controllable and the material to find an answer to the ultimate questions of life and to believe in something which can change one's life in a significant way. Often the people concerned are either not aware of what the church can offer or are put off by what they consider to be a one-sided emphasis on morality or by the institutional aspects of the church.

In summary, one can say that all these symptoms represent many forms of alienation—from oneself, from others, from one's roots and one's culture. The document goes on to state that "people must be helped to know themselves as unique, loved by a personal God, and with a personal history from birth through death to resurrection." It further states that "our pastoral concern should not be one-dimensional; it should extend not only to the spiritual, but also the physical, psychological, social, cultural, economic, and political dimensions."

If you find yourself agreeing with these sentiments, then the question of how to respond in a constructive way becomes critical. It's been my personal conviction for many years that the richness of our spiritual heritage, especially the insights of the Christian mystics, formulate the only meaningful response to the spiritual hunger of the times. These insights from our own spiritual tradition coupled with those of modern science can offer each of us direction in resolving the sense of being lost and set us on the road where we will find meaning.

The title of the Book, *Lift Your Sails: The Challenge of Being a Christian,* indicates that each of us has to do something. It comes from an early Church Father who said that the task we face is to lift our sails and set out on the journey to the Father. I was attracted to this saying because of my sailing experiences, and because it provides such a powerful image. Indeed, we all need to lift our sails, to pull up the anchors that we have put in place and set out on the spiritual adventure of living life, of responding to Christ's invitation to follow him.

Lift Your Sails is the fruit of years of study and research. It is a reflection of my own journey and the journeys of the many people who have graciously shared their own experiences with me. It is an attempt to share with you what has deeply touched my own life, given it meaning, and enabled me to discover what an exciting adventure this life really is.

I ask that you read this book not simply in order to get through it; rather, you should approach it as what is tradition-ally called *lectio divina.* By *lectio divina* I mean that you should first of all put yourself in the presence of God, and then LISTEN. When you feel something in the text touch you especially deeply, stop reading and reflect on it, gently allowing your reflection to deepen into prayer. When your reflection and prayer come to an end, then resume where you left off. You'll find that by listening, reflecting, and praying over the text the integration and insights that you're looking for will come to you in and through the work of the Holy Spirit.

I pray that you'll find it a rewarding experience. The chap-ters provide you with the necessary steps involved in lifting your sails, and when you reach the end I hope that you will have discovered how exciting life can be and that you'll never want to pull those sails back down! In setting out on your journey Christ assures you that you *will* finally reach eternal life; you need only maintain your course through the particular ups and downs he has set before you. If you do so, you can rest assured that, as Walter Hilton says, "in due time you will get there in safety."

1 "COME FOLLOW ME"

WHEN CHRIST SAYS, "I am the Way, the Truth and the Life" (John 14:6), he invites each of us to follow him, to discover the mystery and meaning of our particular journey. It is an invitation to set our course knowing that he will not fail us; we need only keep our sails up so that the Holy Spirit can fill them. This is how we continue to grow in the fullness of the life of Christ. Only he can fill the void within us.

With the growing influence of technology, the materialism from which it springs, and the secularization of modern society which is its result, many people either become dissatisfied with their traditional beliefs, or reject them outright. But no matter how much they ridicule or reject, there remains a profound spiritual hunger. We all yearn to connect with something that transcends the boundaries of our daily existence and gives life meaning. Without this relatedness to the transcendent which surrounds and supports us, our lives have nothing to feed on but the daily joys and pains of work and leisure, tragedy and comedy. And yet we know all too well that without some greater vision beyond the cycles of light and darkness, laughter and tears that we all experience, our lives become increasingly intolerable. When the evening news, *Time* magazine, and the latest economic forecast are our only indicators of reality, life can seem pretty meaningless.

Time and time again, I have seen Christians young and old searching for some light. They want to live lives of integration, of intense witness, but the possibility of that life is overshadowed by what has become an antiquated response to God's invitation to follow him. The church has given them structures, rules, and guidelines which in our present day are no longer meaningful. Such guidelines can often be condensed into nice abstract truths, but they do not explore our potential for true spiritual freedom.

Each of us cries out for the meaning that will allow us to fulfill our potential as human beings. The message of the gospel and the insights of the mystics and saints who responded to Christ's invitation to follow him still provide the answer to this cry. Today, as always, they offer us the opportunity to fulfill our own potential and discover the meaning to which God calls each of us. We need only look again and pose new questions. If we search the scriptures and the writings of the spiritual masters, we can find the light that provides meaning to everyday life in a world that is tossed hither and thither by every kind of wind.

If asked what each of us could do to invite the transcendent back into our lives, I would respond: we must try to cultivate, through reading and reflection, the understanding that our lives are a journey—a spiritual pilgrimage. It is crucial that we see ourselves as adventurers in search of a goal, free to choose our direction if we are to find the fulfillment we seek. This pilgrimage is a search for something that has been lost or hidden, but which is ours in and through baptism—it is our very birthright. Let us now consider the basic elements of this search.

Socrates once said that the beginning of all wisdom is wonder. Unless we learn how to be astonished at the simple fact that we are alive, at the gentle passing of the seasons, at the wonder of our bodies and our minds, we will find it difficult to see our lives as a journey, a pilgrimage, an adventure. We all know that we are on a road that begins with birth and ends in death, but our capacity for wonder depends upon whether we perceive our movement down that road as being along a conveyer belt, or as willful and conscious motion.

We need to reflect upon the passage of time in our lives and the remarkable transformations that are constantly occurring.

Most of us have only a vague sense that we were once children, adolescents, young adults, and so forth. This sense is perhaps punctuated by the memory of a few specific incidents, but if we look more closely we will see that even these memories are, at best, only half memories. We call past incidents to mind but the tone of these memories is too often colored by our present state of mind. A complete memory unfolds only when we recall exactly how our minds worked, how we felt, our attitudes, problems, and struggles—in short, what the world looked like when we were six, twelve, twenty, and so forth. This is not an easy exercise but even an attempt at it brings a sense of the ceaseless transformation of the human soul—an unfolding that usually escapes our notice. Ho hum, we say, and begin another day.

One of the most important things I ever did in my adult life was to go on a journey back to the source of my earliest memories. I returned to my childhood home in Scituate, Massachusetts, a small coastal town south of Boston. I walked along the paths and beaches, and spent time in the places that had so impacted my life; the homes I lived in, the church that was such a special place for me, the schools where I studied, the places where I worked and where I played. I tried to put myself back in time and to recall how the world looked to me then— not for the purpose of judging what I'd become, but just to get a sense of the path my own journey had traced.

This experience was very moving, and I felt once again the joys and sorrows of a person on a journey. I discovered that I had lost many of the qualities I had had as a young person. Qualities like spontaneity, trust, and openness that I once took for granted were, for the most part, no longer part of who I was. I had come to think of many of those qualities as childish, and I was continually reminded that they had to go so that I could grow more fully into the wisdom of "the world." And so, like a lot of people, I began to lose my uniqueness by trying to conform to the expectations of others and becoming absorbed in the values of my culture, which, as I later discovered, had little to do with the Good News of Christ. The poet William Wordsworth mourns this loss of innocence in "Ode: Intimations of Immortality," where he describes the prison bars and darkness that descend upon the heart and eyes as childhood wonder fades.

Of course, the past can never be recaptured. When I speak of exercising memory, it is not in order to live in the past, but to invite the past—and with it, that sense of childlike wonder—into the present. This, of course, is what Jesus meant when he asked each of us to become as little children, which he says is the only way we can enter the kingdom. We must be reawakened to the sheer wonder of our own changing lives and relationships.

Reawakening to this sense that our lives are wonder-filled journeys saves us from what scholars call literalism. Literalism is commonly expressed in such phrases as "Life is nothing but . . ." and "What you see is what you get." People who take such views fail to perceive things symbolically; they're unable to see that above and beyond the events of our lives, yet intimately connected to them, there is a cosmic drama going on—the drama of creation, transformation, and redemption. The mythical traditions of all times and cultures describe this drama. With subtle variations, they all tell the story of an individual on a journey, seeking a new life or a treasure of some sort, and struggling against the forces of darkness in order to achieve liberation, the pearl of great price, or a sacred paradise.

Each of us plays the central role in this drama; it is at once yours, mine, and everyone's; it is individual and cosmic at the same time. Jesus knew this very well and by responding to the deeper, transcendent currents of his own life, he was able to bring about the means of redemption for all of us. We must remember that at least until Jesus left home and began a life of teaching and preaching, he did live a normal, hum-drum life—on the surface. Like each of us, Jesus woke up each morning and faced the ordinary and often demanding tasks that constitute daily life. But for Christ, these daily realities were revelations of his Father's workings, and he took this journey and raised it to another level of meaning. In other words, the visible world, the ups and downs of daily life were for Jesus of Nazareth simply clues and invitations to the invisible world of his Father, whose reality he assured us was far more important than what we usually ascribe to our mundane existence.

Is such a vision of the journey, of the symbolic value of our lives, possible for the rest of us? I once heard the philosopher Alan Watts make a bold and rather crude statement, and yet it contained a great deal of truth. He said that Jesus Christ stands in his glory pointing the way, but instead of going that way most of us have chosen to suck his finger. What he was saying is that most of us pay homage to a set of teachings and to an image; too often, our spiritual practice is just a matter of paying lip service to externals. But the real Christian way is to *internalize* the message of Christ, so that we live it out in our own journey. Cardinal Newman said the same thing as Watts, but a little less audaciously, when he stated that the crucial issue concerning faith is whether you give a merely notional assent, or a real assent. By notional assent Newman meant a "yes" spoken with your head but not with your whole being. All too often, we say "yes" to Jesus, but then refuse to follow or even try to understand the way he reveals to us. Real assent is operational; our "yes" is authentic only when we strive to live it out in our daily lives.

Faith shows us that life is a journey, an adventure into the kingdom that is within us and all around us, for which the visible world and all its realities—our bodies, occupations, trials, and achievements—are merely symbols and clues. Your journey is not just a wandering; it is a pilgrimage towards a goal, a quest. And yet, it's a curious kind of quest, for it is in the searching, not the finding, that we actually discover true meaning. Jesus tells us that the treasure is buried in the field; that field is our lives. To find the treasure is to unearth the source of meaning and richness which faith empowers us to find.

One of the major obstacles to this searching is ordinary human complacency. "Why should I search? Things are going fine. I'm basically satisfied." To tell the truth, the religious wisdom of our heritage can say little to a person who poses this sort of question. Religious teachings make their mature entry, and the pilgrimage begins in earnest, only when we sense that something has been lost or that we are lost. Without a sense of suffering or imperfection, a sense that life is somehow hollow and out of joint, all exhortations to the search fall on deaf ears; the seeds of the kingdom are cast on fallow ground. But if a person senses that behind the ups and downs of daily life, behind the ebb and flow of our energies and interests there lies a more cosmic drama, then perhaps he has ears to hear the call of Jesus.

Not to search is to be content with easy answers, to ignore the mystery, and to say "no" to Christ's invitation to set out on a journey. The spiritual journey is not just another task to be added to your life. This compartmentalized view of spirituality is one of the greatest misunderstandings of our age. No, the spiritual journey reflects God's own generosity, and, as such, it touches *every* aspect of our lives. The secret of its power to do so lies in the fact that it is not just another duty, but rather an attitude, a mode of being that underlies all duties, an understanding that one carries through all the moments of the day. This developing attitude transforms the quality of our lives and opens our eyes to the love of God.

When we discuss these issues, we are posing questions about our commitment to a way of life, an orientation, a direction. We never stop asking the question, and each time we do, we are looking for a yes or a no. You can commit yourself to following Christ or refuse to do so. Theologians call this crossroads the "fundamental option," because it is a choice that deals with the orientations of one's life. If you avoid these questions about belief you will flounder and drift in life. This choice is the fertile ground from which the Christian grows and develops.

Throughout the New Testament the Christian is asked to choose, to make a radical commitment to a relational process of change and development. Christ calls each of us to make this radical decision when he says: "For he who would save his life will lose it; but he who loses his life for my sake will save it"

(Mark 8:35) and "Seek first the Kingdom of God and his justice and all things shall be given to you besides" (Matthew 6:33). The fundamental option, then, is that choice which deals with the totality of one's existence, its meaning and its direction. It brings into play the very essence of a person: the conscious and the unconscious, the rational and irrational—in short, all the facets of one's being. The decision to follow Christ must be radical, a total commitment. In saying "yes" to his invitation to come and follow him, each of us sets out on an exciting adventure.

As I look back on my own journey, I can only say that it surpasses all the dreams I had as a young boy when I first heard his invitation and said "yes." I grew up in a loving family. Of course, my parents had their trials like any couple. But in the end, they paid the price of their "yes" to one another and to Christ—they lived out their commitment. It was in that Christian family setting that I first heard the invitation of Christ. That I saw this invitation as an opportunity to set out on a great adventure is due, I often think, to my Irish heritage. Every Irishman is at heart an adventurer. I was raised in a small town and my home overlooked the ocean, which has been an important part of my journey. I learned to sail when I was a kid and I began to think of my life, my following Christ, as a great adventure. . . . I dreamt I would one day sail across the ocean and bring the Good News to all the world. My mother would often take me to the jetty, which protected the entrance to the harbor, and would teach me to sit still and listen to God in the wind, in the sea, in life, and she would say, "Be quiet and he will speak to you."

He did speak to me, and for a long time in my young adult life, I tried my best to run from him. I no longer went to the jetty to sit and listen—I did not want to hear him in the wind and the sea. . . . It was too painful; he seemed to ask for so much! After many years of struggling to find direction, I entered a seminary, only to leave before ordination; I thought God was calling me to marriage and a family. Shortly afterwards, I was sitting in the darkness of the local church, a place which had always been very special in my life. The lights went on in the sanctuary and the priest appeared with two young people, one of whom was a childhood friend. They were going through the rehearsal for their marriage. Sitting in the dark corner of the church, I once again heard him call, "Will you come and follow me?" This time I knew that he was calling me to the religious life—but it was a vocation I didn't want. I left the church and began to walk the beach. Eventually, I found myself sitting at the base of the light which warned the boats where the jetty was as they entered the harbor, and there again I said "yes."

I broke off my relationship with the girl I had fallen in love with while I was in the seminary, and continued my studies in order to complete my bachelor's degree. Once I'd graduated from college, I started graduate school. But in time, my "yes" began to fade. Once again, I was anxious to escape the commitment I'd made. But it seemed I couldn't run fast enough; he kept after me no matter where I went. Finally, while working in New York as a social worker, I sought out a spiritual director in hopes of resolving my confusion.

At his suggestion, I went to St. Joseph's Abbey, a Trappist community in Massachusetts, to make a retreat and hopefully resolve the question that was haunting me. In the course of the retreat it became obvious to me beyond any possible doubt that God was calling me to the religious life and that I was free to make a choice—it was an either/or decision. I said yes. I entered the monastery. I felt it was the most radical commitment to God I could make. I wanted to let go of everything and give my whole being to him. I saw leaving the world, my family and loved ones, and entering a life of prayer and discipline as an act of complete surrender to his will.

The early days of monastic life were the most difficult. In those days they shaved your hair off, and it seems like I lived from one haircut to another; I would tell myself that if I could just hang on until that next haircut, I'd *have* to stay put, because there was no way I was going to leave the monastery with a shaved head! However, in time I began to love the simplicity of the life and the community. The years seemed to pass quickly, and I grew more and more attached to the abiding peace and joy of monastic life.

Unfortunately, I was diagnosed with rheumatoid arthritis in the late '50s. At first, it was only a mild case, but over the next several years, it grew progressively worse until, in 1967, I had to be admitted to Massachusetts General Hospital. My doctors and religious superiors agreed that the nature of my illness was imcompatible with the austerity of Trappist life and, after discussing the matter further, decided that the best course of action would be to send me to graduate school to earn a degree in theology. In short, I was told that I would have to let go of the life I had grown to love so much. I was devastated. I couldn't understand why God would want me to leave the monastery and return to the world I had surrendered in order to follow him.

In the midst of my anguish, I heard a voice ask, "Why did you become a Trappist?"

I answered, "Because I wanted to give you everything."

"Did you give me everything?"

"Yes," I replied, "what else do I have? I left my family, my loved ones, the world—everything!"

His response changed my life forever. "If you've left everything, then why won't you let go and come follow me?"

I broke down and wept. It occurred to me that, all this time, I only *thought* I was following Christ. The truth was that I was still hanging on to *my* way of doing things; my life was still *my* response to God's invitation. I finally said "fiat"—so be it—you can have it *all*. In that moment, my whole being was filled with a profound inner peace and joy I'll never forget. Once again in my journey, God had spoken to me in and through the events of my life and given me the help I needed to listen and say "yes." This time, I let go and set out never again to know where I was going. I wanted only to be a true pilgrim on a journey, totally dependent upon Christ.

Since that dramatic moment my life has been an adventure, and he has taken me places where I would never have gone of my own choice. Each of us sets out on such an adventure, and we must continually try to listen and respond with our own "yes." And it's crucial to remember that our security can only be found in trusting him with all that we are and have, being certain that he will never fail us.

The journey that each of makes is described in various ways by the mystics. St. John Climacus compares the spiritual journey to climbing the rungs of a ladder. St. Teresa of Ávila uses a number of different images: the seven mansions, the various ways of watering the garden, and so on. St. John of the Cross sees the spiritual journey as comprising three stages, the purgative, illuminative, and unitive. And the author of *The Cloud of Unknowing*—a fourteenth-century treatise on contemplative prayer—states that the Christian life "seems to progress through four ascending phases of growth, which I call the Common, the Special, the Singular, and the Perfect."[1] These phases describe an ever-deepening life of friendship with the Lord.

From the early church into our own times, all of these authors have described growth in the spiritual life as a continuing reaffirmation of our desire to follow Christ, through which we draw closer and closer to him. The mystics point out that there are—indeed, that there must be—obstacles, and that there are some who begin the journey and never finish. They stop along the way and become entangled in comforts and compensations that prevent them from hearing the voice of the Master. Such people find themselves unwilling to pay the price of their "yes"; they lose their sense of direction and begin to drift. But the mystics assure us that the Lord never gives up; even when we fail in our commitment to follow him, he continually reaches out to re-invite us to follow him, and to find real peace in our journey.

Thanks to the various schools of psychology and the social sciences that have been emerging steadily since World War II, we have at our disposal today a wide array of tools for assessing

---

1. William Johnston, ed. *The Cloud of Unknowing* (Garden City, N.Y.: Doubleday/Image Books, 1973), 45.

the moral and emotional development of a person. These sciences, in their attempts to understand the various life stages we pass through, construct models of human growth that are remarkably similar to those formulated by the mystics. When we compare their research with the writings of yesterday's spiritual authors, we find that the latter were indeed grounded in what we now know to be fundamental principles of human growth. However, the mystics did not have the kind of access to information that we have today, and so it becomes essential for us to examine the insights of psychologists and social scientists in order to gain a more profound understanding of the stages of growth. Their findings describe not only these different stages but also the challenges that we must face if we choose to be open to the process of growth.

The Center for Human Development has made extensive use of various psychological theories to facilitate self-knowledge and point up the challenges that the participants in our programs will encounter as they continually reaffirm their own "yes," as they grow into the fullness of their own uniqueness. It is my sincere belief that these theories provide valuable tools that can help us along the course of our spiritual growth, and it would be a terrible mistake to ignore their findings. For example, in *Measuring Ego Development,* psychologists Jane Loevinger and Ruth Wessler offer a highly insightful way of looking at the challenges—and obstacles—we face if we wish to grow toward the fulfillment of our journey. In their study, they describes three developmental stages of personal growth: the conformist, the conscientious, and the autonomous. The first of these is the one in which people all too often get stuck:

> Here the child identifies himself with authority; his parents at first, later other adults, then his peers. This is the period of greatest cognitive simplicity. There is a right way and a wrong way, and it is the same for everyone all the time, or for broad classes of people. . . . Rules are accepted because they are socially accepted, by whatever group defines the child's horizon. Disapproval becomes a potent sanction. There is high

value for friendliness and social niceness. Cognitive preoccupations are appearance, material things, reputation, and social acceptance and belonging. . . . The way things or people are and the way they ought to be are not sharply separated. Hence we have the phenomenon that people describe themselves and others in socially acceptable or, as psychologists like to say, socially desirable terms. People in the conformist stage constitute either a majority or a large minority in almost any social group. . . .

At the conscientious stage inner states and individual differences are described in vivid and differentiated terms. One feels guilty not primarily when one has broken a rule, but when one has hurt another person. Motives and consequences are more important than rules per se. Long-term goals and ideals are characteristic: ought is clearly different from is. . . .

The conscientious person is truly self-critical, but not totally rejecting of the self. . . . He is aware of choices; he strives for goals, he is concerned with living up to ideals and improving himself. The moral imperative remains, but it is no longer just a matter of doing right and avoiding wrong. Moral issues are separated from conventional rules and from esthetic standards or preferences. . . . Achievement is important, and it is measured by one's own inner standards rather than being primarily a matter of competition or social approval, as it is at lower levels. . . .

The autonomous stage is so named partly because one recognizes other people's need for autonomy, partly because it is marked by some freeing of the person from the often excessive striving and sense of responsibility during the conscientious stage. Moral dichotomies are no longer characteristic. They are replaced by a feeling for the complexity and multifaceted character of real people and real situations. There is a deepened respect for other people and their need to find their own mistakes. . . . Striving for achievement is partially supplanted by a seeking of self-fulfillment. In acknowledging inner conflict, the person at this level has come to accept the fact that not all problems are solvable. . . . the autonomous person has the courage to acknowledge, to cope with conflict rather than blotting it out or projecting it onto the environment. The autonomous person has a broader scope; he is concerned with social problems beyond his own immediate experience. He tries to be realistic about himself and others.

In most social groups one will find no more than perhaps 1 per cent, and usually fewer, at our highest or integrated level. . . . Only a few individuals reach the stage of transcending conflict and reconciling polarities that we call the integrated stage.[2]

As Loevinger and Wessler point out, most people progress to the stage of role conformity and remain there. In this stage, they are forced to seek the meaning of life outside themselves; their identity and self-worth are measured by their adherence to external—and often arbitrary—standards. Sadly, their ability to conform can never satisfy their need for genuine self-acceptance and positive self-regard, and their search all too often ends in frustration and despair. The truth is that our growth in this fundamental area takes place primarily in and through the influence of people who can love us as we are. This, as we'll see later on, is a taste of God's unconditional love, which alone frees us from the slavery of conformity and the expectations of others. The center during the past fifteen years has found very few priests and religious at this latter stage, and rectifying this situation is one of the most important challenges the church faces today.

The transition from the conformist to the conscientious stage opens us to difficult choices, and we become aware that life is not "black and white." Those at the conformist stage hold rigidly to rules and laws, as though they contain the ultimate meaning, and are unable to move beyond them in particular situations. But Catholic theology has always taught that every rule, every law in the church has to be based and grounded in one supreme law: the commandment of *love*. Therefore, in certain situations one can actually break a particular rule in order to fulfill the law of love—this is called using *epekia*. It's always been in the books but most of us are scared to death to use it,

---

2. Jane Loevinger and Ruth Wessler, *Measuring Ego Development* (San Francisco: Jossey-Bass, 1970), 4–7.

and because we are unable to assume responsibility for this—because we lack the inner freedom—we often fulfill the obligations of the law but fail in charity.

I recall a good example of this from my childhood. At one time, several of my brothers were very sick and my mother missed mass on Sunday in order to take care of them. My father wanted her to confess this to the priest but my mother refused. She told him that she had an obligation to take care of the kids and shouldn't feel guilty for fulfilling her role as a mother and obeying the commandment of love. Most of us can probably recall such times when we violated some particular rule and felt guilty, even though we knew the rule was subservient to charity.

Also in the conscientious stage we come to accept the fact that we need one another, that we are essentially dependent from birth to death. In this realization, it dawns on us that it is only in and through community—the community of our friends, family, and loved ones—that our growth as human beings is achieved. Those at the conformist stage fail to grasp this fundamental reality. Ironically, their adherence to social convention is a frustrated bid for independence; by living their lives according to external standards, rather than the needs of others, they strive to prove that they don't need anyone!

Those individuals who have found their way to the autonomous stage are able to negotiate the challenges of the journey and have grown to accept the reality of who they are and who we all are—wounded pilgrims on a journey. At this stage, they have finally tasted the unconditional love of the Father—they are free! Until each of us reaches this stage, we cannot know true inner freedom. It is therefore imperative that we do not succumb to the norms of our cultures and the various structures under which we live, but continually strive to follow Christ and be willing to pay the price of our commitment. For he alone is the way, the truth, and the life, and anyone or anything that tries to sidetrack us from him must be rejected, regardless of the cost.

Of course, the center is not unique in drawing on the insights of the behavioral sciences. After Vatican II, there were many peo ple in the church who deemed certain of its doctrines as outdated and repressive, and, so, discarded them. In the midst of the vacuum they had created, some of them fled to the behavioral sciences for solutions. And while many of them learned a great deal from these disciplines, in my opinion they never succeeded in integrating their new insights with their spiritual heritage. Perhaps they never meant to. But for whatever reason, many of them have forgotten that rules and structures do have their place in spiritual formation—they are essential if our aim is to promote growth.

Our work at the Center for Human Development is firmly grounded in the belief that, if we are to assist the people of God in their pilgrimage to the Father, we must integrate our own mystical tradition with the insights of the behavioral sciences into the growth of the individual. But we also recognize that there is a crying need for direction and, yes, even structures that can support members of the church as they respond to Christ's challenge to grow. We can neither throw up our hands and call for a return to the past models of formation nor reject the past and try to build new models outside the context of our spiritual tradition. Our present situation is not one that calls for an "either/or" but rather a "both/and" solution.

The mystics had a marvelous way of framing the most complex matters in a clear and simple manner. Without the aid of any modern pyschological theories and methodologies, *The Cloud* author succeeds in describing the dynamics of our search for God and for growth in language that is at once both lucid and profound:

> For out of all his flock he has lovingly chosen you to be one of his special friends. He has led you to sweet meadows and nourished you with his love, strengthening you to press on so as to take possession of your heritage in his kingdom.
>
> I urge you, then, pursue your course relentlessly. Attend to tomorrow and let yesterday be. Never mind what you have

gained so far. Instead reach out to what lies ahead. If you wish to keep growing you must nourish in your heart the lively longing for God. Though this loving desire is certainly God's gift, it is up to you to nurture it. But mark this, God is a jealous lover. He is at work in your spirit and will tolerate no meddlers. The only other one he needs is you. [3]

God asks you—indeed, he *needs* you—to say "yes" to your own unique journey, a journey that can never be duplicated. There is only one you and your pilgrimage was meant to be an exciting, challenging adventure. But how do you find the path to set out on this journey, this response to Christ's invitation to follow him? In the following chapters we will begin to explore the richness and the immensity of our spiritual heritage. And we'll look not only at the insights of the mystics and saints, but also the understanding of human growth that we've gained from the behavioral sciences.

The winds of God's grace are always blowing; we need only make the effort to lift our sails.

---

3. *The Cloud of Unknowing,* 47.

2 TWO THINGS NECESSARY FOR THE JOURNEY

CHRISTIAN SPIRITUALITY EMBRACES every dimension of our lives. It is our participation in the life of God, the particular way in which each of us listens for the sound of his voice. It is our response to a God who reveals himself to each of us from moment to moment. As such, every person's spirituality is unique to him or her; there may be similarities but there are no duplications.

In the same way, the spirituality of any given age is a unique response to God. It is formulated through the particular events that shape the lives of its people. It is important for us to examine our spiritual forebears' insights into the meaning of the gospel, because once we locate the central themes of their faith—those concerns that bind Christians to one another from age to age—we can then understand what they have to teach us about our own personal and spiritual development. Gleaning the wisdom of our spiritual ancestors allows us to speak to our contemporaries with a freshness that makes the message of Christ relevant and dynamic.

The Cloud of Unknowing provides a perfect example of the ability of a particular tradition to revivify our own spiritual journey. This fourteenth-century treatise on contemplative prayer has found a popularity today which isn't difficult to understand when one considers the spiritual hunger that is all around us. The author has never been identified but scholars generally agree that he was a monk who wished to remain anonymous. In his introduction to *The Cloud,* William Johnston writes:

> It is the work of a man who is friendly, anxious to give help and counsel—a man endowed with keen psychological insight, who knows the human mind, who is aware of man's tragic capacity for self-deception and yet is endowed with a delicate compassion for those who suffer as they struggle to remain in silent love at the core of their being. But his counseling, it must be confessed, is not the non-directive type about which we today hear so much. Rather it is authoritative—the guidance of a man who has trodden the mystical path himself and offers a helping hand to those who will hearken to his words.[1]

Our spiritual tradition flows from one great mystic to another and Johnston goes on to point out the striking similarity of this unknown English mystic with St. John of the Cross, who wrote on the spiritual journey two centuries later. He attributes this resemblance to the unifying power of the Spirit when he writes, ". . . it is the great stream of a common tradition that has formed the minds of these two great men, both being part of a mystical current that has flowed through Christian culture, breaking down the barriers of space and time separating fourteenth-century England and sixteenth-century Spain; nor have its surging waves lost their power in the twentieth century."[2] Like Johnston, I believe that the influence of the Spirit— what he calls "a mystical current"—leads us along the same path as *The Cloud* author and St. John of the Cross. It may speak to us in words that reflect the concerns of our own age, but what it has to tell us is, and has always been, essentially the same.

In one chapter of his treatise, *The Cloud* author tells us that there are two essential virtues we need if we are to see our

---

1. William Johnston ed., *The Cloud of Unknowing* (Garden City, N.Y.: Doubleday/Image Books, 1973), 8.

2. Ibid., 31.

pilgrimage through to the end: *humility* and *brotherly love.*
"Whoever acquires these habits of mind and manner," he tells
us, "needs no others, for he will possess everything."[3] It all
sounds too simple, but it really is true: all that we need to set out
on our journey and to follow Christ faithfully is humility and
love of one another.

Many years ago I read a book by Arthur W. Combs called
Perceiving, Behaving, Becoming, and it had a profound impact
on me. The thrust of this work is that a person's perception
determines his behavior and potential for growth. In other
words, your behavior flows directly from the way you look at
things. Therefore, it is critical for each of us to be in touch with
our view points, many of which were instilled in us at a young
age. And unless we have undergone some radical conversion of
mind and manners they are still there, determining our behavior and affecting—often inhibiting—our growth. For example,
you may have a particular idea of what humility is. When I was
young, I was taught that humility is a virtue, but I thought that
it meant putting yourself down and not accepting compli-
ments. So when someone paid me a compliment, I would
respond with remarks like, "Well, it was really nothing" or "I
could have done better." And the spiritual authors I read seemed
to confirm the wisdom of this attitude. I remember reading a
spiritual book in which the "holy person" described himself as
nothing but dung! "Well," I said to myself, "if he feels that way
about himself, then I must be a *pile* of dung!"

It's important to take a few moments and reflect on
your own perception of humility. What does it mean to you?
Where did you get that understanding? Have you changed your
perception of this virtue at any point on your journey? If so, can
you recall what brought that about? Reflecting on these questions will help you to get further in touch with yourself at this
point of your journey. And, as we proceed to examine *The
Cloud* author's understanding of humility, perhaps it will call

3. Ibid., 64.

you from your present understanding and open you to a new way of perceiving it.

The Cloud author tells us that there are two kinds of humility: perfect and imperfect. In the following passage, we see him discuss the significance of these two types:

> A man is humble when he stands in the truth with a knowledge and appreciation for himself as he really is. And actually, anyone who saw and experienced himself as he really and truly is would have no difficulty being humble, for two things would become very clear to him. In the first place, he would see clearly the degradation, misery, and weakness of the human condition resulting from original sin. From these effects of original sin man will never be entirely free in this life, no matter how holy he becomes. In the second place, he would recognize the transcendent goodness of God as he is in himself and his overflowing, superabundant love for man. Before such goodness and love nature trembles, sages stammer like fools, and the saints and angels are blinded with glory. So overwhelming is this revelation of God's nature that if his power did not sustain them, I dare not think what might happen.
>
> The humility engendered by this experiential knowledge of God's goodness and love I call perfect, because it is an attitude which man will retain even in eternity. But the humility arising from a realistic grasp of the human condition I call imperfect, for not only will it pass away at death with its cause but even in this life it will not always be operative.[4]

Imperfect humility, then, is coming to know ourselves in our woundedness, which is a direct result of original sin, a given. It is essential for each of us to be in touch with this side of our human nature, otherwise our journey will become more and more difficult. *The Cloud* author makes it clear that there is no escape from our inherent woundedness—"no matter how holy we become"! Other mystics have described this knowledge as being painful and difficult to accept. But we *must* accept it; this awareness is crucial to our progress on the journey. In the end,

---

4. Ibid., 65.

we are nothing but wounded pilgrims on a journey to the Father. As *The Cloud* author says, "fast as much as you like, watch far into the night, rise long before dawn, discipline your body, and if it were permitted—which it is not—put out your eyes, tear out your tongue, plug up your ears and nose, and cut off all your limbs; yes, chastise your body with every discipline and you would still gain nothing. The desire and tendency toward sin would remain in your heart."[5]

Later on in his treatise, the mystic elaborates on this point when he writes: "Experience will teach you that in this life there is no absolute security or lasting peace. But never give up and do not become overly anxious about failing."[6] Some of the clam diggers in my hometown had another way of putting it; they used to say, "Look, you were born screwed-up, and you'll be screwed-up until the day you die—so relax!" But they, like the mystics, would reaffirm the necessity to *never give up, never quit.* In our society, we tend to do a great job of helping one another get in touch with our woundedness, our imperfect humility. In fact, I would give you odds that at this very moment, if you have any doubts about your own imperfection, you could put down this book, and if there's someone with you, they'll be delighted to help you progress in this area of self-knowledge! As they say, it's a sure thing.

The other side of the coin—perfect humility—is much more difficult to discover. This type of humility lies in coming to know the unconditional love of God. In *On Loving God*, St. Bernard describes four degrees of the love of God, which we will look at more closely in a later chapter. For now, it will suffice to look at his first degree, which may surprise you. Bernard states that the love of God begins in the love of oneself. This is, in fact, nothing more than the internalization of the gospel, in which Christ reveals his and the Father's love for each of us, *just as we are.*

---

5. Ibid., 64.
6. Ibid., 90.

Let me ask you to reflect on some questions that flow from the gospel and from our spiritual tradition:

Do you believe in God?

Do you believe that Christ became man in order to communicate the unconditional love of the Father?

Do you believe that Christ took upon himself all your faults and sins, and died for you so that you could have life?

Do you believe that you were created in the likeness of God?

Do you believe that God has given you the power to love, to forgive, and to heal?

When I ask these questions I find that most people will answer "yes" to each of them—they believe! But, having said "yes" with their heads, they continue to believe in their hearts that they're worthless pieces of junk. Hence, Bernard would say they've flunked the course. And, sad to say, such people will make little progress on their journey until they come to internalize the message, the Christ event, in their own lives. Each of us must come to know that we are indeed beautiful, lovable persons and that God loves us at this moment, and accepts us as we are—too good to be true, but true!

When I was a young monk and first began to be exposed the writings of *The Cloud* author, St. Bernard, and many others, I was actually astounded by what they had to say about following Christ. For example, no one had ever told me that the first challenge I faced on my own journey lay in coming to accept and to love myself. I recall reading a letter from a monk to St. Bernard in which he went on at length about how much he loved Bernard and God. Bernard replied that it was impossible for the monk to love him, let alone God, since he had not yet learned to love himself. His words, when I first read them, shattered a lot of my preconceptions about the spiritual life and helped me to start opening myself to the real challenges of growth.

There is a favorite spot of mine at the abbey, an old well on top of a hill, where I used to go to think about things and pray. From there, I could look out across the hills and the fields to the monastery in the distance. One day, I had gone there to reflect on the meaning of love, and as I sat there I became aware that whenever anyone had something good to say to me, I would immediately brush it aside with some comment like "Oh well, I could have done much better," or "If you really knew me you wouldn't say that." As I thought about this, I realized that I had somehow gotten into the habit of rejecting the good things that people said to me, and accepting the remarks they made about my faults and weaknesses without question. And as I sat there, I had to wonder, "How did this ever happen?"

The answer came to me in a somewhat humorous way. My attention was drawn to an old cow barn where I had many times shoveled the manure from the cow stalls to the end of the barn, and then opened a trap door that had been set in the floor to dump the manure into the manure spreader below. Suddenly, the lights went on and I exclaimed, "My God, I've spent my whole life under that trap door— no wonder I have such a smelly self-image!"

I began to drift back into the past, and I recalled that in growing up in the "Harbor Irish" section of Scituate, the grownups had always tried to make sure that we would never become proud, since no one wanted us to go to Hell. And so, they all did their part in helping us to be grounded in what *The Cloud* author calls imperfect humility. My father felt that I had a responsibility to shape up and be perfect at whatever I was doing, and he was pretty good at opening the "trap door" on me. I can remember saying the *Memorare* before the statue of the Blessed Mother in our church one day, and as I was leaving I felt good about myself and thought, "Well, the Blessed Mother loves me, and Mom loves me most of the time, so I guess I'm not so bad." As it turned out, I ran into one of my brothers on the way home, who informed me that I was in trouble, even with Mom!

I had plenty of trap door experiences when I was young. When I went off to school I could never seem to draw correctly and my Palmer penmanship left a lot to be desired, so I often found myself staying after school and then walking home, having missed the regular school bus. When I reached my third year of high school everyone agreed I had no future in education, having flunked so many subjects, not to mention all the times I'd been expelled, so on my seventeenth birthday I was sworn into the United States navy.

Strange as it might seem, it was in the navy that I began to see myself in a different light. I was accepted into submarine service and then discovered that I'd been rated in the top five percent of my group, which meant that I had an above average I.Q. and was psychologically well-balanced. I remember one of my Abbots once saying to me that the monastery was something like being in submarine service. I replied that there was one big difference—we were carefully chosen for submarine service!

Despite all the navy did for my sense of self-worth, I eventually left because I'd begun to feel I wanted to give my life to God as a priest. I entered and left the seminary twice, finally convinced that I didn't have a vocation. I attended and graduated from St. Anselm's College in New Hampshire, where I had done well academically and had been deeply touched by the monks. Their care, concern, and encouragement made a lasting impression on me. I continued my studies in graduate school, but I made the decision to enter the monastery before completing my degree. By then my self-image had come a long way from the days of my youth, and I'd begun to accept myself and to believe that I was a lovable human being.

When I entered the monastery I assumed that in such a loving community I would no longer have to experience the trap door. However, I soon discovered that in the Chapter of Faults the trap door was open several times each week, only now it was in the form of fraternal correction—rooted in love and the desire to assist me in my growth! Call it by any name, the end result was the same; the manure was continually coming down on my head. As I sat there on the well, I found myself thinking, "Well, this is just me, no one else has these kinds of problems."

But when I left the monastery and went to Catholic University, I began to work with priests and discovered that they too were experts on opening the trap door on one another. All you had to do was walk into a room of priests and the trap door would open on you. Granted, it usually took place in the form of a joke, but the effect was always the same—the manure had fallen on you. In fact, in order to control how much manure would fall on you, you would learn to open the trap door yourself. I concluded that this must just be a trait of priests, but then I began to work with nuns and I discovered that the Sisters too were very good at opening the trap door; however, they at least did it with a smile! I began to feel that this was probably just a part of religious life, but then in working with lay people I found that they too were well-skilled at opening the trap door.

In short, experience has taught me that most of us have spent at least some time under the trap door. What we need to do now is shut the trap door and nail it down—forever. The Chapter of Faults is gone, along with many of our old methods for chastising one another. However, we've come up with new ways and when someone approaches you and says, "I'd like to give you some feedback," or, "I'd like to share my feelings with you," you can be sure, most of the time, the trap door is about to open on you—so be careful!

After I completed my doctorate, I accepted an appointment to the faculty of the University of North Carolina at Charlotte where I taught in the School of Human Development and Learning. It was there that I became interested in the so-called human potential movement. At that time, research in this field indicated that most of us operate at only 8–16 percent of our potential. Needless to say, this was alarming news, and millions of research dollars were being spent on exploring the causes and discovering how to release this untapped potential. One of the major blocks, it was determined, is *poor self-concept.*

I found this extremely interesting in connection with St. Bernard's first stage of the love of God. Bernard, in the twelveth century, and without a research grant from Louis VI, had discovered through reflection and prayer on the Scriptures that a positive self-concept was essential for the spiritual journey. Bernard certainly didn't have the depth of understanding that we have today concerning self-image, but he did know that our experience of the gospel message is inauthentic if it doesn't create a positive self-regard within each of us. He also understood that adopting this positive self-image is not an easy task; in fact, it is usually a slow process with plenty of ups and downs.

As I've reflected on this, I've come to believe that we foolishly direct almost all of our energy toward helping one another to be rooted in the knowledge of imperfect humility. But, as *The Cloud* author points out, there is also a perfect humility, and each of us must come to know and taste both imperfect and perfect humility in order to make the journey. In his discussion of perfect humility, *The Cloud* author writes that "sometimes people well advanced in the contemplative life will receive such grace from God that they will be suddenly and completely taken out of themselves and neither remember nor care whether they are holy or sinful. . . . though they may lose all concern for their sinfulness or virtue, they do not lose the sense of God's immense love and goodness and therefore, they have perfect humility."[7]

I remember one particular day when I was feeling down and discouraged, thinking that I wasn't worth much; all I could see was the negative side of things, and my faults and weaknesses were like a tremendous weight around my neck. In that moment of despair, I felt the presence of Christ in a very special way, saying to me, "Hey, wait a minute . . . I knew you in your mother's womb; my Father sent me to take your sins and faults to myself and to die on the cross in order to free you; I sent the Spirit to be with you. We dwell inside you and are with you all the time. I told you my mercy endures forever, my love is steadfast. I have the hairs of your head numbered, I know you by name. . . ." and on and on, until I finally broke down and cried, wondering, "Why can't I really believe?"

---

7. Ibid., 65–66.

Perhaps you've never had such an experience, but let me ask you to take a few moments, put the book down, and reflect on your own journey. Think of the times you've hated yourself and believed that you were worthless. Where are you now? Do you believe in your worth? Do you believe in the crazy, unconditional love that God has for you? That it's a *given*, with no strings attached? What will it take to get you to believe in the absolute miracle of Christ?

"Come follow me" is an invitation that you've probably heard and responded to. But, perhaps, like myself, there have been times on your journey when you turned off your "hearing aids" and ignored his invitation, times when you chose to walk to the tune of another drummer. We can explore the true meaning of this invitation by reformulating it as two separate questions: "Will you be my friend?" and "Will you love one another?" In other words, at the heart of accepting Christ's invitation to follow him is our ability to enter into true friendship with him and with one another.

My own views on friendship have been shaped by the writings of two Cistercian saints, Bernard of Clairvaux and Aelred of Rievaulx. And in our own time, the words of Pope Paul VI, especially in his encyclical, "Paths of the Church," have shown me new ways of looking at the life of friendship. The writings of all these authors resonate with one another in affirming that the whole gospel is ultimately founded on love. Jesus spoke of only one commandment as specifically his: "This is my commandment, that you love one another as I have loved you" (John 15:12). And St. John reminds us that "if we love one another, God abides in us and his love is perfected in us" (1 John 4:12). Reflecting upon this message of Christ, theologian Karl Rahner has stated that the love of God and man are ontologically the same. That is, in loving my neighbor I love God, whether or not I advert to it consciously.[8]

---

8. Karl Rahner, "The Unity of Love of God and Love of Neighbor," *Theology Digest*, vol. 15, 87–93.

The mystics continually remind us that God speaks to us in two ways: directly and indirectly. In other words, he can appear to you with a choir of angels and look at you—eyeball to eyeball—and tell you that he loves you, just as you are! Or, he can transmit this same incredible message in and through the people and events he sends into your life. I guess most of us would prefer that he come down with a choir of angels and thus make it impossible for us to ever again doubt our beauty, but the normal way that we come to know his crazy love for us is through our friends, family, the community we live in, and the church. We'll further reflect on the life of friendship in a later chapter, but for now, it suffices to say that we need to be more keenly aware of how we touch one another, especially those who are close to us.

For Christ is not just a historical figure—he *continues* to live in and through each of us. We are all, therefore, reliving the paschal mystery in our own journey. We are free to receive or reject the Christ event in our own lives. But if we choose to receive and internalize the Good News, we are empowered to communicate the unconditional love of God, and set out on the road to an ever deeper positive self-concept and inner freedom— the freedom of the children of God! The question you must ask yourself, then, is, where are you? Do you communicate the love within you? And are you open to receiving love from others?

A major turning point in my own understanding of the importance of communicating took place around the time of my graduation from Catholic University. My father had come to Washington with some of the other members of my family to see me receive my diploma. The graduation ceremonies were scheduled to take place outside, and since it was expected to be a very hot and humid day, I'd arranged for the family to watch the ceremonies from inside an air conditioned building that gave them a great view of everything. But my father decided that he wanted to stay outside, so he stood under a tree by himself and watched the ceremony. When it was finished I walked over to him. I was wearing academic robes over my clerical suit, both symbols of the achievements that were a big part of my father's dreams for his children. He'd always hoped that one of us would become a priest, and that we would all get graduate degrees. Well, there I was fulfilling both of his aspirations for us—and as a kid I'm sure I'd seemed the one least likely to do either—so when I reached my father, I said, "Well, Dad, did you ever think I'd make it?"

He answered, "Oh, of course I knew you'd make it!"

I was surprised, to say the least, and said to him, "Really?"

Of course, when I confronted him like that, he had to come clean. "Well, to tell you the truth, it's a miracle!"

Once again, the trap door was thrown open and down came the manure! But then the rest of my family joined us and we went off to celebrate the "miracle." I returned to Scituate with the family and after a few days my father invited me to walk with him along the beach. As we were walking together I noticed that the tide was out, and there were people digging clams out on the flats. It brought back old memories and I turned to my father and asked him if he remembered all the times he used to say to me, "If you don't shape up, you'll be nothing but a clam-digger!" Clam-digging in those days was about the lowest thing you could do (today it's a lucrative business). He had no difficulty remembering, and I went on to share with him how deeply that had hurt me as a young boy. It was even worse when he would say it in front of Mom. She never said anything when he did, so I began to believe that both of them felt I couldn't do much else with my life.

Well, my father was shocked when I told him all this. "Well, look at what you've done with your life," he said. "You're a priest, you've got your doctorate, and now you're going off to teach at a major university. Your mother and I always knew you had the gifts and talents to do just about anything you wanted, but when you were young you didn't do a damn thing; you flunked your courses and you were always fooling around. And I *had* to motivate you; and thank God I *did* motivate you because if I hadn't, you'd be out there digging clams right now!"

I turned to my father and I told him that it hadn't motivated me; on the contrary, it had led me to believe that I wasn't worth much and probably couldn't accomplish much. He turned to me and asked if I knew that he and my mom both loved me no matter what happened. Without any hesitation I said, "No, Dad, I didn't know that."

That was the second time I saw my father cry. The first was when Mom died. And here again, after so many years, I saw tears rolling down the cheeks of this old man, and with a broken voice he said, "You dummy!" He finally took off his glasses and dried his eyes and asked me, "When did you ever come to us and we weren't there for all you kids?"

"You were always there for us," I admitted.

"Do you remember when you were young and I lost everything in the Depression? Did you kids ever go without anything—didn't you always have food, clothes, a place for you and your friends?"

"Yes, Dad, you both were there, and the sacrifices that you made were obvious to all of us."

"Then how come you didn't know that we loved you no matter what happened—whether you became a priest, a doctor, or even a clam-digger? Didn't you know we loved you no matter what happened?"

It was a bitter moment for me, having to turn to this great man and say, "Dad, I never knew it because you and Mom never told me—you never *said* it."

My father was taken aback by this and replied, "But, we said it by doing all those things for you!" It felt awful, admitting that I hadn't heard the "Good News" of their unconditional love for me, that it just hadn't penetrated my heart.

I told my father that I needed some time alone, and walked out to the breakwater at the entrance of the harbor. He headed back in the opposite direction while I returned to one of my favorite spots from when I was a boy. When I'd reached the end of the jetty, I sat down and began to reflect on all that had taken place between my father and me. I looked out at the sea thinking, "Isn't this a crazy world; here this old man had all this love for me, and the world told him not to say how much he cared." As my thoughts unfolded, it began to seem that culture was the real culprit—my father had been raised to believe that it wasn't all right to express love openly. In my opinion, far too many of us have given ourselves over to cultural values, just like my dad—and left the Good News by the wayside in the process.

This story really touches a nerve for a lot of people. You'd be surprised—or maybe you wouldn't—at how many people hear it and tell me it was my fault that I didn't get the message. "Your parents *did* express their love for you in the things they did," these people insist, "you were just too stubborn to hear it." But it's important to realize that we're all unique. What might get through to one person doesn't necessarily get through to another. Anyone who has children knows this to be true; no two are alike. It seems to me that if we really believe in this great power God has given each of us—the power to love uncondi- tionally—then we need to find a million ways to communicate it effectively to those whose lives have touched our own.

The point of this story is that it's terribly important to com- municate our feelings to one another, and to be consistent in checking to make sure our message is being received. I find it hard to understand why we can't just say to those whom we really love, "Do you know how much you mean to me?" When we take someone we love to a meal, give them a present, pay their college tuition, or whatever, we should ask them, "What does this say to you, about you?" Simply asking the question gives the other person the opportunity to internalize the gift of our love, and that love is nothing less than God's love.

I'm often reminded of a young friend of mine who once told me how he told his girlfriend he loved her when they were around other people. He'd simply ask her, "Do you know what?" The answer, of course, was "I love you," but she'd know what he was feeling as soon as he asked the question. And it's the same question I raise to everyone who has entered and touched my life: "Do you know what?" I remind them that no matter what happens to them on their journey they need only close their eyes and they'll hear me whispering, "Hey, do you know what?" If they believe that I love them as they are, I can make sure that they don't stop there but go on to the real question: "What does my love tell you about *his* love for you?"

The Cloud author maintains that imperfect humility must always precede perfect humility. He states this clearly in the following passages:

> Although I speak of imperfect humility it is not because I place little value on true self-knowledge. Should all the saints and angels of heaven join with all the members of the Church on earth, both religious and lay, at every degree of Christian holiness and pray for my growth in humility, I am certain that it would not profit me as much nor bring me to the perfection of this virtue as quickly as a little self-knowledge. Indeed, it is altogether impossible to arrive at perfect humility without it.

> And therefore, do not shrink from the sweat and toil involved in gaining real self-knowledge, for I am sure that when you have acquired it you will very soon come to an experiential knowledge of God's goodness and love. . . .

> I wanted you to appreciate the excellence of perfect humility so that you might keep it before your heart as a spur to your love. This is important for both of us. And finally, I have troubled to explain all this because I believe that just knowing about perfect humility will in itself make you more humble. For I often think that ignorance of humility's two degrees occasions a good deal of pride. It is just possible that a little taste of what I have called imperfect humility might lead you to believe that you were already perfectly humble. But you would be badly deceived and, what is more, have actually fallen into the foul mire of conceit. And so, be diligent in striving for this virtue in all its perfection. When a person experiences it, he will not sin, then nor long afterward.[9]

Perhaps you've experienced both sides of the coin of humility. Like myself, you may have been grounded in imperfect humility,

---

9. *Cloud of Unknowing,* 66–67.

but as *The Cloud* author points out, this opens us to the possibility of coming to know and taste perfect humility—the unconditional love of God.

As many of us consider the lessons we inadvertently received as kids in cultivating imperfect humility, it's easy to blame certain individuals—whether our parents, relatives, teachers, or whoever— for letting us down by not being thoughtful enough. But this kind of fault-finding is ultimately self-defeating, because we can't attain to the freedom of Christ until we're able to let go of the past. This is another lesson that was brought home to me through a particular experience.

One of my brothers had just built a beautiful home overlooking the sea and the family decided to get together for an open house. We had a genuine New England clam bake, with lobsters, steamers, corn on the cob, the works. I was sitting on the porch, looking out at the sea with my father. The occasion was a deeply moving one for Dad, and he turned to me and said, "Isn't it great that this kid is starting out in life with this beautiful home—he's starting off where I finished!" He went on to tell me how happy he was to have lived to see all of us grow up, to see his grandchildren. And then he talked about how sad he felt when he thought of Mom who had died when we were young and never got to see how things worked out; she was only there for the hard times and all the difficulties that go with raising children. My father was caught up in all the joys and regrets of the day when one of my brothers appeared on the porch, and said, "Well, here are the two main problems of my life!"

Like a lot of Irishmen, my father had a quick temper, and if you got him angry, he could cut you to shreds in a moment. So I immediately began to think of how I could prevent an argument that might spoil the whole family reunion. But before I could say anything, my dad turned to my brother and said, "Well, let me tell you something, and if your mother were here she'd say the same thing. You see, your grandparents weren't perfect and when we came along, we certainly weren't either. We probably made a lot of mistakes with all of you, but now it's your turn, and I pray to God that at least you'll make new mistakes—don't make the same ones we made. So don't waste your time blaming me, your mother, brother, teachers, the priests, or whoever—just get on with your life. And remember to make new mistakes!" My brother turned and left without saying word.

My dad wasn't always so good at conflict resolution, but that was one of the most profound things I ever heard him say. And what he told my brother that afternoon was absolutely true; it's crucial that we learn to make new mistakes. We can't—nor should we—ever hope to stop making mistakes altogether. As I've pointed out, we cannot come into the fullness of spiritual growth until we realize that we're all just wounded pilgrims, and this realization necessarily entails accepting our natural imperfection. But it is important that we leave the mistakes of the past *in* the past. There's no return in dwelling on what could or should have been. True humility asks us to let go of the past and keep our hearts and minds focused on our journey as it unfolds in the present. We will make mistakes, but as long as they are *our* mistakes, we can be certain that Christ will only use them to draw us closer to our goal.

The winds of God's grace are always blowing; we need only make the effort to lift our sails.

3 LOVE OF ONE ANOTHER

IN THE PREVIOUS chapter, we focused primarily on the first of what *The Cloud* author maintains are the two things necessary for our spiritual journey. You may have wondered in the course of your reading why he puts humility before love. There is an old Latin saying, "*Nemo dat quod non habet,*" which translates, "You can't give what you haven't got." Within the context of our present discussion, this means that unless we have first acquired the virtue of humility, it is impossible to love others according to the commandment of Christ. For remember, true humility allows us to love ourselves as God loves us, *as we are.* Without this humility, our feeble attempts to love inevitably come with strings attached. Whether consciously or unconsciously, we place conditions on the love we offer to others. Often we experience hurt and rejection as we try to reach out and love others, demanding that they fulfill every conceivable need that we have. But this is not love. We cannot find love without first embracing both imperfect and perfect humility. This experience leads us through the awareness of the light and darkness that dwells within us to an honest appreciation of who we are. It is from this ground alone that we can enter relationships that call us to love and be loved.

In *The Four Loves,* C. S. Lewis sets before us a clear picture of the challenge we face in learning to love authentically:

> If the Victorians needed the reminder that love is not enough, older theologians were always saying very loudly that (natural) love is likely to be a great deal too much. The danger of loving

our fellow creatures too little was less present to their minds than that of loving them idolatrously. In every wife, mother, child and friend they saw a possible rival to God. So of course does Our Lord (Luke 14:26).

There is one method of dissuading us from inordinate love of the fellow-creature which I find myself forced to reject at the very outset. I do so with trembling, for it met me in the pages of a great saint and a great thinker to whom my own glad debts are incalculable.

In words which can still bring tears to the eyes, St. Augustine describes the desolation in which the death of his friend Nebridius plunged him (*Confessions* IV, 10). Then he draws a moral. This is what comes, he says, of giving one's heart to any-thing but God. All human beings pass away. Do not let your happiness depend on something you may lose. If love is to be a blessing, not a misery, it must be for the only Beloved who will never pass away.

Of course this is excellent sense. Don't put your goods in a leaky vessel. Don't spend too much on a house you may be turned out of. And there is no man alive who responds more naturally than I to such canny maxims. I am a safety-first creature. Of all the arguments against love none makes so strong an appeal to my nature as "Careful! This might lead you to suffering."

To my nature, my temperament, yes. Not to my conscience. When I respond to that appeal I seem to myself to be a thousand miles away from Christ. If I am sure of anything I am sure that His teaching was never meant to confirm my congenial prefer-ence for safe investments and limited liabilities. I doubt whether there is anything in me that pleases Him less. And who could conceivably begin to love God on such a prudential ground– because the security (so to speak) is better? Who could even include it among the grounds for loving? Would you choose a wife or a friend–if it comes to that, would you choose a dog–in this spirit? One must be outside the world of love, of all loves, before one thus calculates. Eros, lawless Eros, preferring the Beloved to happiness, is more like Love Himself than this.

I think that this passage in the *Confessions* is less a part of St. Augustine's Christendom than a hangover from the high-minded

Pagan philosophies in which he grew up. It is closer to Stoic "apa-thy" or neo-Platonic mysticism than to charity. We follow One who wept over Jerusalem and at the grave of Lazarus, and, loving all, yet had one disciple whom, in a special sense, he "loved." St. Paul has a higher authority with us than St. Augustine–St. Paul who shows no sign that he would not have suffered like a man, and no feeling that he ought not so to have suffered, if Epaphroditus had died (Philippians 2:27).

Even if it were granted that insurances against heartbreak were our highest wisdom, does God Himself offer them? Apparently not. Christ comes at last to say, "Why hast thou forsaken me?"[1]

In this passage, Lewis describes some of the influences— Victorian romanticism, St. Augustine, Stoicism—that have impacted our own views on love. When we read history we sometimes deceive ourselves into thinking that we've outgrown the various misconceptions of the past. But on the contrary, our own ideas flow out of the past and, whether consciously or unconsciously, we are affected by the views and concepts of bygone days. One of the great blessings of studying history is that it allows us to look at the past objectively. In doing so, we learn to stand by those views that nurture our spiritual growth, and let go of the ones that inhibit it. For whatever we choose to do—whether to hold on or let go—we are the ones who pay the price for our views and how they affect our daily lives. Each of us has his or her own view of love and it is well worth the effort to examine it and make sure that it's what we really want. We must own our views and beliefs, and this is only possible through reflection and prayer. Of course, we're entirely free not to do so, but we run the risk of living our lives according to principles that aren't grounded in the love of Christ.

I often hear people who are faced with the necessity of changing their views say, "Well, I guess everything I did in the past was wrong." However, the truth of the matter is that as we proceed on our journey we are accountable only for the light we

---

1. C. S. Lewis, *The Four Loves* (New York: Harcourt, Brace, 1960), 136–38.

have. There's no point in dwelling on the mistakes we've made; our only task is to nurture our potential for growth. The fact that the Holy Spirit is alive in the church, continually revealing the deeper meaning of the gospel, and enlightening us through the advances of the various sciences makes it imperative that we be continually willing to let go of old habits and change. If we look at the vast amount of knowledge that is constantly being made available today, it's just plain silly to think that we should have already known everything we needed. We can only follow the light we have at each point of our pilgrimage. So don't worry about what you don't know; as long as you're willing to change when necessary, you're on the right path and the Holy Spirit won't fail you.

Many of us have had to undergo tremendous changes in how we see ourselves and the world over the course of our lives. Those of us who are older can recall a time of little change and, hence, great stability, while a lot of kids today feel that everything is "up for grabs," that everything changes. As I look back on my own life, I can remember a time when everything seemed clear-cut; a question led to a neat little answer and then to a period—that was it. And God help you if you had another question! In those days the difference between right and wrong seemed simple, and there are some people who would like to return to those times—wipe out everything that has taken place since then, and return to the basics. Then, they think, we'll all feel secure again.

I recall the first time I was confronted with the decision to change. I say decision because God never forces us to change or to grow—he leaves us free to respond or not to, and for me it was quite difficult. During my basic training in the navy we were assembled one day for a lecture by the chaplains. The Catholics went to one hall and the Protestants to another. At one point in the lecture, the chaplain told us that we could eat meat on Friday and my immediate reaction was, "I must be in the wrong hall!" After the conference I approached the chaplain in order to make sure he was a priest. When I asked him, he responded, "Yes, I'm Father O'Malley." He then reassured me that I could eat meat on Friday, because we'd been given a special dispensation as servicemen. Well, the first time I ate meat on Friday, I still had a hard time; in fact, I went back to the priest afterwards to make sure it was all right! Some of you can probably remember the difficulties you faced when changes took place in church doctrine; for example, the change in the Eucharistic fast from midnight; the change allowing us to drink liquids before Communion; changes in the rules of abstinence and fasting, and changes in the liturgy. Some of these changes we welcomed with open arms, while others involved traditions that were more sacred to us personally, and therefore gave us great difficulty. Most of us are quite adept in picking and choosing the areas we want to change. However, we must always be willing to let go of the past and remain open to the voice of the Holy Spirit as it speaks to us through the church and through the ordinary events of our lives. When we do look back, we should be able to say, "I tried to follow the light that was given to me." That's all that is needed, and all that any of us are capable of doing. The journey is a constantly unfolding mystery. Through it, we grow into the fullness of the life of Christ. And we can always depend on him for the light we need to follow him—he will never fail us!

Perhaps, like me, you can identify things that you once held to be infallible, only to find later on that you'd changed your view. It is important to realize that the principles behind our ideas and actions don't change. However, as we grow in our understanding of them—and as we change in response to all the other factors that shape our lives—we see the need to change how we *apply* those principles. The fact is that the Spirit is constantly providing us with new insights into the message of Christ. These insights allow us to bring the Good News to the world with freshness and new meaning, rather than through the often dated views and expressions of the past.

It is indeed amazing, when one thinks of the impact of faith on our lives, that so few people spend time keeping abreast of this very important area of their lives. We often attend work-shops, lectures, and seminars to keep abreast of our chosen occupations. How much more should we be willing to keep abreast of present day interpretations of the gospel and its sig-nificance in our daily lives? My brothers are all professional men and very competent in their respective fields, but it con-tinually amazes me to hear them say to my nephews and nieces, when discussing religious issues, "Go ask your uncle," or better still, "I can't explain it. I just believe!" It's not all their fault. Certainly, one of the major responsibilities facing the church today is in helping the laity—not to mention priests and reli-gious—to grow continually in their ability to articulate the Good News in the "marketplace."

St. Paul puts it another way when he speaks of the need for transformation (Galatians 3:27). He tells us that in every trans-formation something is left behind, but something is also gained. In this statement, he indicates that there are two dimen-sions of every Christian's journey, a journey that can be seen as the commitment to a life-long process of conversion. One of these can be described as negative, in that we are asked to let go of views, values, and habits that once held meaning for us. The other is positive, in that the new views, values, and habits that replace the old bring us to a deeper freedom, with which we can more fully respond to God as he reveals himself to us through our daily lives.

We each grow up in an environment that has its own pecu-liar psychological, sociological, and cultural factors which can either open up or constrict our view of the world around us. We breathe in various biases and prejudices as we grow up—and each society has its own—until they are a part of us. When this happens, they tend to block us; they prevent us from seeing life in its broader dimensions and become obstacles to our spiritu-al journey. We continually find ourselves driven to find the right way, the "how-to," and a lot of energy can be wasted this way. Karl Rahner writes that there is no recipe for living the Christian life, no static definition of the gift that the Spirit grants to the individual. "All that is possible," says Rahner, "is to perceive vocational imperatives. The response of the Christian embraces some form of asceticism (discipline) which enables him to become free. Free, not in order to wall up his heart but to give it away, to God and to the world."[2]

Whether you call it conversion, transformation, or a shift in perspective, it all boils down to the fact that we are called to grow, and all growth involves letting go! Of course, this letting go *does* require discernment; we should be careful not to simply abandon ourselves to the changing tides that are continually carrying our culture in one direction or another. But at the same time, we must always be ready to let go of whatever prevents us from entering into a life of perfect freedom in Christ. In short we must let go, but with discernment; we must surrender ourselves to the will of God while always holding fast to the wisdom he grants us through the Spirit.

Sometimes, when I'm searching for insight, I pick out an author whom I respect, and let the book just open to any page and begin to read. On one of those occasions I found myself picking up Cardinal Newman's *Sermons and Discourses*. The book opened to his sermon on the feast of St. John, in which he discusses Christ's injunction to love all men equally. Newman points out that it's impossible to simply start loving everyone equally. Instead, we must begin by loving individuals, especially the people who are close to us, and in loving them, begin to reach out to others. If we can maintain this course, Newman tells us, by the end of our journey we will have reached the point where we can love everyone equally. It is only in taking the risk to love individuals that we can begin to touch the entire world.

Lewis makes a similar point when he disagrees with St. Augustine and others who would caution us against letting ourselves love too deeply:

---

2. Karl Rahner, *Theological Investigations*, vol. 3 (Baltimore: Helicon, 1967), 84–85.

There is no escape along the lines St. Augustine suggests. Nor along any other lines. There is no safe investment. To love at all is to be vulnerable. Love anything, and your heart will certainly be wrung and possibly be broken. If you want to make sure of keeping it intact, you must give your heart to no one, not even to an animal. Wrap it carefully round with hobbies and little luxuries; avoid all entanglements; lock it up safe in the casket or coffin of your selfishness. But in that casket–safe, dark, motionless, airless–it will change. It will not be broken; it will become unbreakable, impenetrable, irredeemable. The alternative to tragedy, or at least to the risk of tragedy is damnation. The only place outside Heaven where you can be perfectly safe from all the dangers and perturbations of love is Hell.[3]

I imagine many of us can identify times when we tried to love in a safe way, or as they used to say in the church, "supernaturally." This attempt to be safe usually arises from the times that we have, as they say, "fumbled the ball"—we've made mistakes in relationships and gotten hurt in the process. There are times when we think we are loving, only to discover that we are really operating out of our own needs, out of selfishness. All of this constitutes the ordinary way that we grow in self-knowledge, and it takes both failures and successes to learn and grow in the art of love. The hurt that we do encounter comes from various sources, but most often from the knowledge and experience that we either have not loved, or when we have loved that our love has not been accepted. Needless to say, relationships of love can sometimes involve betrayal of secrets and confidences, which causes us great pain. At these times, we can tragically fall into the trap of building a wall around ourselves to protect us from ever again being hurt, misunderstood, or rejected. Sadly, when we succumb to this temptation we are—to paraphrase Lewis—living in a hell of our own design.

It's safe to say that we would all like to become great lovers, free to love and be loved, free from our wounded selves, and above all possessing every virtue which would ensure that our

---

3. Lewis, *The Four Loves*, 138–39.

love was always "pure and beautiful." Some people decide to wait until they've put all the pieces together before they'll risk loving. But Lewis cautions us against trying to exert too much control over the course of our love:

> I believe that the most lawless and inordinate loves are less contrary to God's will than a self-invited and self-protected lovelessness. It is like hiding the talent in a napkin and for much the same reason. "I knew thee that thou wert a hard man." Christ did not teach and suffer that we might become, even in the natural loves, more careful of our own happiness. If a man is not uncalculating towards the earthly beloveds whom he has seen, he is none the more likely to be so towards God whom he has not. We shall draw nearer to God, not by trying to avoid the sufferings inherent in all loves, but by accepting them and offering them to Him; throwing away all defensive armour. If our hearts need to be broken, and if He chooses this as the way in which they should break, so be it.[4]

In his classic *On Spiritual Friendship*, Aelred of Rievaulx tells us that love is bound up in friendship, and that the Christian life is essentially a growing into freedom and the perfection of friendship. Book One is written in the form of a dialogue between himself and a monk named Ivo. When, in the course of their talk, Ivo translates the Gospel of St. John, "God is friendship," Aelred does not hesitate to add, "He that abides in friendship, abides in God, and God in him."[5] For Aelred held out little hope for those who could never respond to the invitation of friendship and enter into what he calls "a most sacred kind of love." St. Bernard and St. Aelred both saw how important friendship was in grounding one's life and in growing into the fullness of the Christian life. To refuse the love of another, or to accept that love without giving in return, inevitably brings death to the soul.

I think that every pilgrim longs to experience the fruits of friendship, but many of them are unwilling to pay the price.

---

4. Ibid., 139.

5. Aelred of Rievaulx, *On Spiritual Friendship*, trans. Mary Eugenia Laker, S.S.N.D. (Kalamazoo: Cistercian Publications, 1977), 65–66.

Jesus reveals to us in the Gospel of St. John what friendship really is and what price we must pay for it. He says that he chose us (John 15:16), indicating that friendship is first and foremost a *choice*. He also tells us that we are friends rather than servants because he has revealed everything to us. He has been completely open and shared with us all that is his (John 15:15). What is it to be a friend? Jesus says that real friendship involves a radical commitment. "A man can have no greater love than to lay down his life for his friends" (John 15:13). And finally, he tells us how we must respond to his gift of love and friendship: "You are my friends if you do what I command you. . . . This is my commandment, that you love one another as I have loved you" (John 15:12–14).

Like Jesus, we are all free to choose another and offer them our love and friendship, leaving them free to either accept or reject the invitation. When the other responds in freedom and accepts the gift that we offer, then we begin the process of sharing all that we are, and so follow the model given to us by Christ. There is a wonderful rhythm to this process of sharing, a mutual listening and responding as the relationship unfolds from one moment to the next. It is what in earlier days they called the art of love and friendship.

True love and friendship, though we all long for it, is indeed scary, since it involves a radical commitment. This radical, total commitment that Jesus calls us to is the reality that one must be willing to lay down one's life for a friend. This brings friendship, love of one another, out of the realm of the temporary—there can be no "here today, gone tomorrow" where friendship is concerned! Friendship involves a total commitment. Antoine de Saint Exupery makes this point in his deceptively simple *The Little Prince*: "You become responsible, forever, for what you have tamed [i.e. loved]."[6] Every time I tell someone that I love him or her, I have in fact put my life on the line—not just for a

---

6. Antoine de Saint-Exupery, *The Little Prince*, trans. Katherine Woods (New York: Reynal & Hitchcock, 1943), 72.

moment, while it feels good, but forever! I am literally saying to that person, "I am willing to respond to you with all that I am and all that I have." The only boundaries or limitations on this relationship are those of our respective vocational commitments. True, we cannot always be for another what we would like to be, or what they might want us to be, due to the other responsibilities that we have assumed in our lives, such as marriage, priesthood, or religious life. Nonetheless, true friendship flowers in that environment that we provide for one another, an environment of trust and honesty.

Not long ago, I read that current research shows that 87 percent of men report that they have "never experienced intimacy." I found this shocking and yet perhaps it shows us why there are so may divorces and broken homes in our society today. Women do much better than men in this area of their lives, and perhaps this reflects the influence of our cultural values, which encourage boys to be macho. This emphasis tends to put men out of touch with the feminine side of their personalities, and they lose their ability to express their deepest feelings.

I recall that when I was a young boy it was normal to sit in my father's lap, to kiss him, and he was comfortable in throwing me up in his arms and catching me, hugging and kissing me—expressing the love he had for me. However, when I reached adolescence, he announced that men didn't do those things, that we expressed our love for one another with a pat on the back, or a firm handshake. I'm sure it all seemed perfectly normal to him, but what it meant was that a lot of the intimacy I'd once had with him was gone. On my seventeenth birthday, when I was sworn into the navy, he walked with me to South Station in Boston to catch the train for basic training. When it came time to say good-bye I wanted to embrace him, and I could feel the tears welling up in my eyes. But before I could do or say anything, he extended his hand and said, "This was your decision and I expect you to live up to it—God bless you!" And then he was gone.

When I got on the train I began to cry; I was having a hard time trying to be a man, trying to hide my pain from all the other young men who were with me. I never found out how my father dealt with his feelings, but I feel certain that he cried that day too. It took me a long time to realize that I needed to let go of the macho ideal, and get in touch with the feminine side of my own personality. There is no one who is purely masculine or feminine; each of us possesses characteristics of both. The challenge for each of us is to become comfortable with ourselves, to take ownership of all our qualities that flow from our masculinity *and* our femininity. It's a difficult challenge and one that I still struggle with. I remember once a college student came to see me and he began to cry. Without thinking, I said, "Pat, don't cry!" He looked up at me and said, "Vince, what's wrong with crying?" I had to laugh at myself, and I told him to go ahead and cry all he wanted to, that it was beautiful that he could express himself that way.

Intimacy is essential for each of us. But there are too many people today who confuse intimacy with sex, only to discover that one doesn't automatically lead to the other. It's true that sex can be an expression of intimacy, but is isn't necessary for intimacy. In Book Three of *On Spiritual Friendship,* St. Aelred writes, "There can be love without friendship, but friendship without love is impossible."[7] What he was getting at is that friendship entails much more than love; it entails intimacy. Intimacy, for St. Aelred and many other mystics, is the deep sharing that takes place between *friends;* as St. Ambrose says, "a friend hides nothing." No doubt, at this very moment, you can identify individuals whom you love but with whom you would not share everything, for whatever reasons. On the other hand, with a friend you are comfortable sharing whatever you feel, knowing that your confidence will be respected and appreciated.

One of the major challenges the church faces today is in once again becoming a school of love and friendship. Pope Paul VI makes this point in his first encyclical where he describes the need to cultivate the art of spiritual communication. Love of

---

7. *On Spiritual Friendship,* 91.

one another, friendship, is an art! It is developed and perfected
through disciplined practice, in learning from mistakes, in
being open to honesty, and in meeting the challenge to grow.
Aelred extols the virtues of this art in language that is nothing
short of fervent:

> . . . scarcely any happiness whatever can exist among mankind
> without friendship, and man is to be compared to a beast if he
> has no one to rejoice with him in adversity, no one to whom to
> unburden his mind if any annoyance crosses his path or with
> whom to share some unusually sublime or illuminating inspi-
> ration. "Woe to him that is alone, for when he falls, he has none
> to lift him up" (Eccles. 4:10). He is entirely alone who is with-
> out a friend.
>
> But what happiness, what security, what joy to have someone
> to whom you dare speak on terms of equality as to another self;
> one to whom you need have no fear to confess your failings;
> one to whom you can unblushingly make known what progress
> you have made in the spiritual life; one to whom you can
> entrust all the secrets of your heart and before whom you can
> place all your plans! What, therefore, is more pleasant than so
> to unite to oneself the spirit of another and of two to form one,
> that no boasting is thereafter to be feared, no suspicion to be
> dreaded, no correction of one by the other to cause pain, no
> praise on the part of one to bring a charge of adulation from the
> other. "A friend," says the Wise Man, "is the medicine of life"
> (Sir 6:16).[8]

St. Thomas Aquinas once wrote that all love of God is based
on analogy. What he meant was that we love God only to the
extent to which we love one another. Or, as Aelred writes,
"friendship is a stage bordering upon that perfection which
consists in the love and knowledge of God, so that man from
being a friend of his fellowman becomes the friend of God,
according to the words of the Savior in the Gospel, 'I will not
now call you servants, but my friends' (John 15:15)."[9] For

---

8. Ibid., 71–72.
9. Ibid., 73.

Aelred, Thomas, Bernard, and so many other mystics and saints, the ultimate question for each of us was, "How do we relate to one another?"

Which one of us, at some point or another, hasn't been disappointed to see what he thought was friendship come to an end? When this happens there is a great deal of pain, and we often wonder how we failed, or what we could have done to preserve the relationship. However, as Aelred points out, true friendship can never end:

> . . . a friend is called a guardian of love or, as some would have it, a guardian of the spirit itself. Since it is fitting that my friend be a guardian of our mutual love or the guardian of my own spirit so as to preserve all its secrets in faithful silence, let him, as far as he can, cure and endure such defects as he may observe in it; let him rejoice with his friend in his joys, and weep with him in his sorrows, and feel as his own all that his friend experiences.

> Friendship, therefore, is that virtue by which spirits are bound by ties of love and sweetness, and out of many are made one. Even the philosophers of this world have ranked friendship not with things casual or transitory but with the virtues which are eternal. Solomon in the *Book of Proverbs* appears to agree with them when he says: "He that is a friend loves at all times," manifestly declaring that friendship is eternal if it is true friendship; but, if it should ever cease to be, then it was not true friendship, even though it seemed to be so. . . . remember this: he was never a friend who could offend him whom he at one time received into his friendship; on the other hand, that other has not tasted the delights of true friendship who even when offended has ceased to love him whom he once cherished. For "he that is a friend loves at all times" (Prov. 17:17). Although he be accused unjustly, though he be injured, though he be cast in the flames, though he be crucified, "he that is a friend loves at all times." Our Jerome speaks similarly: "A friendship which can cease to be was never true friendship" (*Letters,* 3:6).[10]

Today, we tend to use the term friendship loosely, and I think that many of the difficulties we encounter in this area are

---

10. Ibid., 55–56.

due to the fact that we don't fully grasp the commitment and responsibility that go with friendship. From the fifth to the twelfth century, the Celtic tradition referred to a true friend as a "soul friend." There was a saying in those days that a person without a soul friend was like a body without a head. And needless to say, it's pretty hard to make any progress on the journey without a head!

Today most people distinguish between different kinds of friendship, and the same held good in Aelred's time. In *On Spiritual Friendship* he writes that there are three categories of friendship—carnal, worldly, and spiritual. The first two are often mistaken for true friendship. However, individuals who try to assuage their hunger for intimacy by entering the gate of carnal relationships will find only tragedy—they become broken human beings living, as they say, from one high to the next. They are driven by lust and a misplaced desire to satisfy their needs for affection. People become objects in such relationships, something to be enjoyed and then thrown away. There is no honesty, no commitment, and certainly no responsibility to the other person. Most of us have experienced such relationships at some point on our journey, and know how empty and meaningless they are.

However, such experiences can allow us to emerge as stronger and wiser human beings than we were, and help us to get on with what our lives are meant to be. My old abbot used to say that there are two ways of learning: one is to sit at the feet of a master; the other is through experience. The ideal is to embrace both of these ways, but I must confess that in my own life I have learned mostly from experience, especially my mistakes.

The other type of imperfect friendship is the worldly relationship. Here, we encounter the "fair weather friend," and the person who fosters relationships with others in order to use them. In such a relationship, one is regarded as an object which the other can use to profit financially, socially, or in any way that will assist him in achieving his goals. This kind of relationship is often more difficult to detect than the carnal, and often, one won't know of the nature of the relationship until the "friend" has gained what he wanted and walked out of the relationship. Of course, such experiences leave scars and can leave us feeling confused and suspicious. When this happens, we must be careful not to put up a wall to protect ourselves. If we do, we run the risk of shutting out the people who are true friends.

We usually experience both carnal and worldly relationships at some point, but if we can learn from them, they will help us to continue our search for the real thing—spiritual, soul friendship—with renewed strength and discernment. The gate is indeed narrow and few seem to find their way to it, but when we do succeed in passing through it, we enter into the pastures where we discover at last the flowering of our efforts to love one another, the richness and beauty of soul friendship. Here are found the meaning, fulfillment, and deep inner peace that come from following the voice of the Master:

> . . . a friend praying to Christ on behalf of his friend, and for his friend's sake desiring to be heard by Christ, directs his attention with love and longing to Christ; then it sometimes happens quickly and imperceptibly the one love passes over into the other, and coming, as it were, into close contact with the sweetness of Christ himself, the friend begins to taste his sweetness and experience his charm. Thus ascending from that holy love with which he embraces a friend to that with which he embraces Christ, he will joyfully partake in abundance of the spiritual fruit of friendship, awaiting the fullness of all things in the life to come.[11]

Our spiritual tradition in the area of friendship is indeed exciting and challenging. I recall as a young monk when I was first introduced to the writings of Aelred by the prior of my monastery, Father Edward McCorkle, how difficult it was to end our discussions. Often, I was too excited to wait for our next meeting!

---

11. Ibid., 131.

Many years have passed since then, and I still find myself returning to these works and pondering them over and over again. Each time, they leave me feeling inspired, challenged, and full of hope. However, to internalize the wisdom of the saints in this area is the work of a lifetime. As I've said, the way is filled with mistakes and little failures. But no matter how many times you feel tempted to quit, it's imperative that you keep pushing ahead. If you do, I know that one day you'll discover the pearl of great price, true friendship. When you arrive at that stage of your journey, you'll know that in soul friendship you have found everything. The hurts, mistakes, betrayals, and everything else that has happened to you on the journey will seem like nothing. Indeed, it is worth a million betrayals to find a true friend.

I think Aelred's assertion that you can have love without friendship, but never friendship without love says a lot about the necessary preparation for marriage today. I remember a young man who met me one evening for dinner to talk about his divorce. As he spoke with me, I became aware that there hadn't been any real friendship between his wife and him. At the same time, it was also clear that he did love her, and this caused considerable difficulty for his wife, who couldn't make sense of their divorce in light of this fact. I shared with him Aelred's comment that friendship always entails intimacy, whereas you can love someone without intimacy. His eyes lit up and he said, "That's it! We were never friends!" It seems to me, as I reflect on that conversation, that marriage is above all a call to a life of soul friendship, and we need to help young people see this. And those who are already married need help in supporting their relationships and perfecting the "art" of friendship and spiritual communication.

Today we hear such expressions as "falling in love" or "I love you" pretty frequently, but in many cases, such phrases are just describing strong feelings of affection for the other person. It may even be love; but all too often, it is *not* friendship. On this point, Aelred writes:

> We embrace very many with every affection, but yet in such a way that we do not admit them to the secrets of friendship, which consists especially in the revelation of all our confidences and plans. Whence it is that the Lord in the Gospel says: "I will not now call you servants but friends" (John 15:15); and then adding the reason for which they are considered worthy of the name of friend: "because all things, whatsoever I have heard of my Father, I have made known to you.". . . From these words, as Saint Ambrose says, "He gives the formula of friendship for us to follow: namely, that we do the will of our friend, that we disclose to our friend whatever confidences we have in our hearts, and that we be not ignorant of his confidences. Let us bare to him our heart and let him disclose his to us. For a friend hides nothing. If he is true, he pours forth his soul just as the Lord Jesus poured forth the mysteries of the Father" (*Duties of the Clergy* 135). Thus speaks Ambrose. How many, therefore, do we love before whom it would be imprudent to lay bare our souls and pour out our inner hearts! Men whose age or feeling or discretion is not sufficient to bear such revelations.[12]

Like St. Aelred, I think that true friendship is the ability to "stand naked" before one's friend. There are no hidden secrets; we are comfortable revealing both the dark and the light sides of our personality to the other.

Of course, you probably know from experience how scary that can be. This is because of the incredible power we give to the other—the power to accept and affirm us, and at the same time, the power to reject and seemingly destroy us. Therefore, we are tempted to confine our relationships to the lighter side of who we are; we make small talk; we discuss common interests; we have a good time at the bar. We enjoy being with one another, but all the time we avoid anything that would touch the real depths of our being. Aelred argues that this type of friendship "is to be tolerated [only] in the hope of more abundant grace, as the beginnings, so to say, of a holier friendship. By these beginnings, with a growth in piety and in constant zeal for things of the spirit, with the growing seriousness of maturer

---

12. Ibid., 112–13.

years and the illumination of the spiritual senses, they may, with purer affections, mount to loftier heights from, as it were, a region close by, just as yesterday we said the friendship of man could be easily translated into a friendship for God himself because of the similarity existing between both."[13] In other words, we can and should cultivate these more superficial friendships into authentic, soul friendships; in so doing, we enter into the boundless freedom of friendship with the Lord.

Love is indeed a powerful force and it always leads to some expression of our affection. In dealing with our affections, we must try to ensure that they flow out of respect for one another, and we must find in the relationship that vehicle which is both proper and fitting to communicate our love. One must always be attuned to oneself, the other, and the unfolding of the relationship from moment to moment if the communication of affection is going to be an affirming experience. When one finally embraces a true friend, a soul friend, then and then alone does one experience and taste the depths and fullness of the Christian way of life. "This is true and eternal friendship, which begins in this life and is perfected in the next, which here belongs to the few where few are good, but there belongs to all where all are good."[14]

As *The Cloud* author says, humility and love of one another are the two things that we need to make the journey to the Father. The journey begins at birth, and continues through death to the resurrection, and during that pilgrimage each of us, in his or her unique way, relives the paschal mystery. Yes, the life of Christ is relived in us. We are given the freedom to respond to his invitation at each and every moment of the journey as the paschal mystery unfolds in our lives. And, as *The Cloud* author says, "the only other one he needs, is you"—to continually say "yes!" You will fall, make mistakes, and yes, even sin; but as long as you never quit, you can rest assured that God will bring you to the mountain and you'll see that what St. Paul says is true, that "all things work together for good for those

---

13. Ibid., 114.
14. Ibid., 111.

who love God" (Romans 8:28). As I so often say, it's too good to be true, but true!

The journey can be long and no doubt there will be times when you feel discouraged. My old abbot used to say to me that it's important to tie a knot at the end of the rope, and when you reach the knot—that is, when you feel like you've reached the "end of your rope"—hang on and don't let go! Don't give way to discouragement. Just put your trust in the Lord, he won't fail you. Each day brings new opportunities and by continuously striving, we will finally win.

Monsignor Dwyer, my spiritual director before I entered the monastery, was a true master, and I later discovered that the old abbot considered him to be one of the finest spiritual directors on the East Coast. He is now retired, but will always be a part of me, and over the years I've tried to share with others the wisdom that he opened to me. He once said to me that there was only one question you needed to ask on your journey: "Am I trying?" Never worry about whether you are succeeding. That question is one of our society's greatest obsessions, but it has nothing to do with the spiritual life, since success depends upon situations, circumstances, other people, and God himself—none of which you have any control over.

Nor should you waste time regretting the past; you can't shine the light you now have on a time when you didn't have it. It took me a long time to digest this simple rule, and I can only urge you to learn from my own experience, that if you indulge either of these worries—your success and the past—the trap door will open, and the manure will come down on your head! Hold on to the one valid question: *Am I trying?* If you can keep responding to that question with a "yes," you'll one day find yourself on the mountain, viewing everything from a different perspective, and you'll come to understand these words of Paul: "all things work together for those who love God."

The winds of god's grace are always blowing; we need only make the effort to lift our sails.

4 THE LIFE OF DIALOGUE

HUMILITY AND LOVE of one another are the ground, the very foundation from which we are called to live out the gospel. Through the centuries, the church's directives have been rooted in her basic desire to see each of us embrace the total message of Christ and to judge all things according to the gospel. Each generation, however, faces the task of making the message of Christ relevant, for once again as Rahner says, "Truly realized Christianity is always the achieved synthesis on each occasion of the message of the Gospel and of the grace of Christ, on the one hand, and of the concrete situation in which the Gospel is to be lived, on the other"[1]

As we look at our lives, we cannot escape the simple fact of change. We are free to give or withhold our assent to its call, but we can't deny its existence. And each of us is challenged to remain open to it so that we can grow in the course of our journey. Today, as perhaps never before, we live in the midst of changing attitudes and circumstances, and we must come to accept this fact. In our relationships with one another, with the world we live in, and with God, we must always be open—open to new ways, new insights, and new life.

The history of salvation clearly indicates that we are always left free to make choices, to orient our lives in one direction

---

1. Karl Rahner, *Theological Investigations,* vol. 3 (Baltimore: Helicon, 1967), 139.

rather than another. But how we exercise this freedom is absolutely critical, as Louis Monden points out in *Sin, Liberty, and Law*:

> The choice among many objects offers an infinite number of possibilities; the fundamental option is made between a "yes" and a "no" in which man, as a spirit, unconditionally commits or refuses himself. That option always amounts to letting oneself go: either yielding to a "becoming," to a growing towards a more perfect self-realization, or falling back on an already acquired self-possession, rejecting the advance in self-realization and the new risks. In order to realize itself this basic option must enter into a dialog with a complete psycho-physical situation and development, assume all acquired determinisms within its free directedness and thus bestow on them, out of that freedom, a new shape for the future.[2]

To paraphrase Monden, when we yield ourselves to the *principle* of becoming, that principle integrates all of the people, situations, and events that define the course of our lives, and from them creates a new freedom, with new opportunities for self-realization. Of course, making this fundamental choice can be a little scary. It's like turning down an unfamiliar road; we don't know where it will lead us. But if we're willing to take that risk and put our trust in this principle of becoming—which is in fact nothing less than the Holy Spirit—it will shape our journey in ways that surpass our own hopes. When we consider the matter in this light, we can see that this basic choice is essential to our fulfillment. If we don't make it, we can only flounder and drift through life.

This option is the ground from which the Christian grows and develops. Revelation tells us of the intimacy to which God calls us, but in order to enter into that intimacy we must choose this crucial "fundamental option." It is this basic commitment we refer to when we speak of conversion. It places each of us in

---

2. Louis Monden, *Sin, Liberty, and Law* (New York: Sheed & Ward, 1965), 31.

a dynamic relationship, wherein we are initiated into a state of grace and communion with God. Throughout the New Testament we are asked to make this decision, to enter into the process of change and development.

A choice is free only when it springs from a deeper source than ordinary human actions. A truly free choice draws on our entire being and alters the very course of our lives. As I mentioned earlier, one of the major problems in our society is that people avoid making a fundamental choice because of the commitment it involves; either consciously or unconsciously, they know they will have to pay a price for their choice. What they don't realize, however, is that a price will also be exacted for their refusal to make this choice, their unwillingness to make a commitment.

For those of us who have chosen to follow Christ, all of our options can be narrowed down to a single choice, between a life of love and a life of selfishness. If we put this choice within the framework of relationships, we must choose to pursue either the path of soul-friendship or the path of carnal or worldly relationships. In the Scriptures we are invited to enter into such a soul-friendship with God. He speaks to each of us in the Scriptures, and we reply to him in faith. Faith is our response to a living God who discloses himself to us from moment to moment in everyday life. Life, then, is a dialogue with the God who lives in each of us and calls us to community with one another in him.

The word *dialogue* has become rather common these days. In the past, its principle meaning was the exchange of words among characters in some sort of narrative, such as a play or poem. As such, dialogue was artificial in that it was controlled by the artist. Within the present context, however, dialogue is not artificial. In fact, it represents the very antithesis of artifice. It is the medium through which we communicate to one another all that is authentic in our experience. As such, the term carries deep religious significance.

True dialogue unites people who long to be united. It is realized in the authentic, loving encounter between people who want to be made one. Pope Paul VI, in his encyclical *Paths of the Church* uses the term to challenge today's Christian and highlight the relevance of the gospel to the modern world:

> The duty consonant with the patrimony received from Christ is that of spreading, offering, announcing it to others. Well do we know that "Go, therefore, make disciples of all nations" (Matthew 28:19) is the last command of Christ to His apostles. By the very term "apostles" these men define their inescapable mission. To this internal drive of charity which tends to become the external gift of charity we will give the name of dialogue, which has in these days come into common usage. . . . See then, Venerable Brethren, the transcendent origin of the dialogue. It is found in the very plan of God. Religion, of its very nature, is a relationship between God and man. Prayer expresses such a relationship in dialogue.[3]

In this document, Pope Paul not only challenges us, but shows us how to bring wholeness and meaning into our lives: it is in and through lives of dialogue. This dialogue begins for each of us at birth and ends when we are united with God in eternal life. Dialogue, then, is the vehicle that allows us to discover true friendship, first with God and then, through him, with one another.

The greatest achievement of Vatican II was that it revived a spiritual richness that had been lost for some time—the understanding that the church is not an institution or a system of beliefs, but simply the people of God. There was a time when the church was described as a school of love or friendship. In this school, we learn the art of dialogue, what Pope Paul also refers to as "the art of spiritual communication." This art is crucial because it is the means through which we give and receive the unconditional love of God. God himself teaches us this art so that we can grow in the fullness of his life within us.

---

3. Pope Paul VI, *Ecclesiam Suam (Paths of the Church)* (Washington, D.C.: National Catholic Welfare Conference, 1964), 29–31.

The training of the dialogical person begins at home. When you look back on your childhood, however, you might find that dialogue is something there didn't seem to be enough of. Such a lack of dialogue in the home can have disastrous effects on us. I can recall a time when I was young that I began to worry that I was an orphan. One day, I decided that there was nothing for it but to run away from home. So I packed a few things and got ready to leave. When my mother saw me walking down the staircase with my little bag, she came up the steps and stopped me.

"Where are you going?" she asked.

"I'm running away from home," I replied.

With that, she sat down on the stairs and pulled me next to her. "Why are you running away?"

"Because I'm an orphan."

"And what makes you think you're an orphan?"

I then proceeded to explain to her that all my brothers had blond hair and blue eyes, and therefore I knew that I didn't belong to her and Dad.

"And what color hair do I have?" she asked.

"Brown."

"What color eyes do I have?"

"Brown."

"You see, you look like me—you have brown hair and brown eyes. Your brothers all look like your father." And then my mother told me that she'd nearly died giving birth to me. Unfortunately, when she finished sharing that with me, all I could say was, "I don't believe you." And with that, I proceeded with my grand exit. Fortunately, it was cold and snowing, and I returned shortly after to a warm hug.

You can probably remember times when someone who cared for you tried to reach out and enter into dialogue with you, but, like me, you couldn't or wouldn't open yourself to the depth of love that the other person was offering you. No matter how many such opportunities we miss, however, we are still invited to take up the challenge of developing the art of spiritual communication.

Each of us struggles to establish true dialogue in our lives, and in every family—the primary school of love and friendship—there are successes and failures. As we proceed to examine the principles of dialogue, reflect periodically on your own journey and try to identify both the times when you entered into dialogue with others and the good things that resulted from those encounters. And do make a point of looking at the positive experiences. Too often we tend to focus on the encounters that felt like failures. Remember, watch out for that trap door! If you do find your attention drawn to a disappointing experience, be sure to ask yourself: What did I learn?

Pope Paul writes that "we need to keep ever present this ineffable, yet real relationship of the dialogue which God the father, through Christ in the Holy Spirit, has offered to us and established with us, if we are to understand the relationship which we, i.e. the Church, should strive to establish and to foster with the human race."[4] In other words, as God reveals himself and enters into dialogue with each of us, so too must we strive to engage this same dialogue with and through one another.

Christ teaches us by telling stories. One of the greatest challenges that each of us faces lies in getting in touch with his own story and learning to share it. God has chosen to continually re-enact the paschal mystery in each of our lives. He makes himself present in each of us and asks us to reveal his presence to one another through the stories that describe the uniqueness and authenticity that he ordains for each of his people. I am unique and can never be duplicated; the same is true of you. It is in and through our uniqueness that God reveals his beauty, his love, his mercy, and his steadfastness. And he calls us to reveal our uniqueness to others, that they might see and understand the power of God in their own lives.

I am constantly amazed at the power we have to touch others and to encourage them by sharing our stories. Over the years, so many people have approached me to tell me how

---

4. Ibid., 31.

deeply it touched them when I shared my own stories with them. They tell me that they feel as though they know me, but more often than not, they "met" me on a television or video screen. It just goes to show what a powerful means for communication storytelling can be; it offers us the opportunity to encounter one another in a deeply meaningful way. And it invites others to share their own stories, which further reveals the work of God in their lives. Sure, it's risky, but if we're willing to take that risk and respond to the invitation of self-revelation, we are given the power, in and through the process, of revealing the beauty of God within us. Of course, we can choose not to enter into this process, but if we do so, we effectively refuse to manifest to others the beauty and power of God that has been entrusted to us from all eternity. And that would indeed be sad.

In *Paths of the Church* Paul VI sets out six fundamental principles for the life of dialogue which he drew from his meditation on the Scriptures. These principles describe the manner in which God enters into dialogue with each of us and, by extension, show us how to dialogue with one another and the world. The first principle is spontaneity, which is grounded, like all of the principles, in God's very being: "The dialogue of salvation was opened spontaneously on the initiative of God: 'He loved us first' (I Jn. 4:10). It will be up to us to take the initiative in extending to men this same dialogue, without waiting to be summoned to it."[5]

Spontaneity is crucial to the life of dialogue. However, I can remember a point in my life when I realized I'd lost the ability to be spontaneous. I think a lot of us come to this sad realization somewhere along the way in our journey. For most of us, it comes from growing up in a culture that smiles at spontaneity in children and frowns on it in adults. As we grow older, many of us are taught to put a damper on our spontaneity in the fear that it might lead us to make mistakes.

---

5. For all quotations on Paul VI's six principles, see ibid., 31–33.

Today, however, research indicates that if we can act more from the impulses and intuitions of our inner selves, it is more conducive not only to our own growth but to the growth of others. One need only reflect on this for a moment to see that it's true. Does it really touch you when you receive a postcard from someone who has taken a trip and you know that you are on their list, and that the address label and perhaps even a line or two were already finished, waiting only for the stamp and postmark from their destination? Or, does it touch you when, out of nowhere, you receive a card from someone who just happened to think of you and wanted you to know? I'm sure you'll agree that it's in those spontaneous movements of the Spirit that we touch one another, not programmed activities!

And yet, it's a real challenge to rediscover this childlike quality. In fact, you can learn a lot about the life of dialogue simply by observing children. Christ tells us that unless we become like children we cannot enter the kingdom. Spontaneity is essential to the life of true dialogue, and though at times it might feel awkward, we need to get in touch with our inner selves and learn to operate from those spontaneous movements.

The second principle of dialogue, according to Pope Paul, is charity. The dialogue of salvation begins with charity, with the goodness of God: "'God so loved the world as to give his only begotten Son' (Jn. 3:16); nothing but fervent and unselfish love should motivate our dialogue."

The third principle describes an interior attitude that is somewhat foreign in our culture, which tends to be result-oriented: "The dialogue of salvation," writes Paul, "was not proportioned to the merits of those to whom it was directed, nor to the results which it would achieve or fail to achieve: 'Those who are healthy need no physician' (Lk. 5:31); so also our own dialogue ought to be without limits or ulterior motives."

So often it happens that we enter relationships in order to get results or to fulfill our own needs. When we give in to these motives we remove ourselves from dialogue, and the results are always frustrating. I remember something my father used to say to us when we were kids: "You're all individuals, you're all different, and it would be foolish to compare you to each other. All I ask is that you do the best you can—your effort is what's important." It was sound advice and I took him at his word. When I showed him my report card at the end of the school term, I reminded him that I had tried. He took one look at the report card and said, "Well you didn't try hard enough, and you're grounded!" I learned the hard way that results did matter—in fact, they mattered a lot. As I grew up, this lesson was brought home to me time and again. Sometimes I can't help but be gratefully amazed that so many young people manage to see that true friendship can't be found through selfish behavior, like demanding results and success.

I think that as we grow older, most of us find it easier to see the wisdom of our parents' actions, or at least to appreciate that they did the best they could. It is indeed a very difficult job, trying to strike a balance between the innocence of the child and the experience of the parent. But if we become weighted too heavily towards experience—if we start to think that producing results and succeeding are essential, then we'll suffer a great deal. For there is much more to life than success and tangible results. Christ came into the world to assure us that God's love for us is unconditional, and this is a message we must allow to settle deep within our hearts. For it is only through this interior experience the knowledge that God loves us as we are that we attain real freedom. And when we have realized this freedom, we enter relationships based on real love, relationships in which we don't make any demands upon the other. It requires tremendous discipline, but the payoff is, needless to say, out of this world!

The fourth principle of dialogue is the necessity of leaving other people free to accept our reject our invitation to enter into dialogue:

> The dialogue of salvation did not physically force anyone to accept it; it was a tremendous appeal of love which, although

placing a vast responsibility on those toward whom it was
directed (cf. Mt. 11:12), nevertheless left them free to respond
to it. . . . So too, [our dialogue] will not be introduced in the
armor of external force, but simply through the legitimate
means of human education, of interior persuasion, of ordinary
conversation, and it will offer its gift of salvation with full
respect for the personal and civic freedom.

When you reflect on this principle you might discover, as I did,
that in many of your relationships you do not leave the other
person totally free. I know I often do. Every time I enter a relationship, I find that I'm looking for some kind of response from
the other person, and if I'm not careful, the gift I give will come
with strings attached. Then, when I want that response I simply
pull on the string to get it. But there's an old saying that if you
tie a single string to the leg of a bird, it won't be able to fly. It is
our task to let people fly by setting them free. I've gotten into
the habit of carrying a pair of "mystical scissors" on my own
journey. When I discover that there are strings attached to my
love for another person, that I'm trying to use them to meet my
own needs, I pull out my scissors and cut them loose. For it's
only in the environment of freedom that we can grow into the
fullness of our unique gifts.

Each of us is called to create an atmosphere of invitation. As
the kids say (or at least, as they used to say), we need to "put out
good vibes" so that others can perceive our invitation to relationship and choose to accept or reject that invitation in an atmosphere of pure freedom. It takes discipline to leave the people we
care for entirely free to respond to us as they like, but it's the only
circumstances under which real relationship can take place.

The fifth principle reminds us that our love cannot be
exclusive but must be open to all. "The dialogue of salvation,"
writes Pope Paul, "was made accessible to all; it was destined for
all without distinction (cf. Col. 3:11); in like manner our own
dialogue should be potentially universal. . . ."

Sometimes I find it difficult to be open to those who are
close to me, let alone to complete strangers. When I reflect on

our world today, where people so often pass each other like ships in the night, never really acknowledging one another's presence, I'm convinced that our society needs to grow in its capacity for openness. This growth has to begin with those who are close to us. When we've learned to be open with the people who are most intimately involved with our lives, we can begin to extend the circle outward, gradually opening ourselves to the entire world.

I travel a great deal and I have to admit that I often want to bury myself in a book or just close my eyes rather than be open to the person sitting next to me on the airplane. Wearing a Roman collar can be like flashing a neon sign that says, "Step right up and tell me what's on your mind!" and I've often wished I were in secular dress. Still, I must also admit that it's always an unforgettable experience when someone reaches out to me, and I'm willing to be open to them. At those times, I feel that God put me in that airplane seat just so I could be there for that person. It's terribly important to remember that we are not ships that pass in the night; even when we are strangers, we can conduct ourselves as brothers and sisters who care about each other.

The sixth principle, like the third, poses a challenge to our cultural belief in the importance of success:

> The dialogue of salvation normally experienced a gradual development, successive advances, humble beginnings before complete success (cf. Mt. 13:31). Ours too will take cognizance of the slowness of psychological and historical maturation and of the need to wait for the hour when God may make our dialogue effective. Not for this reason will our dialogue postpone till tomorrow what it can accomplish today; it ought to be eager for the opportune moment; it ought to sense the preciousness of time (cf. Eph. 4:16). Today, i.e. every day, our dialogue should begin again; we, rather than those toward whom it is directed, should take the initiative.

We live in a society that puts a great emphasis on success, and this pressure has a major impact on our self-image. However, Paul VI points out that the life of dialogue does not depend on our success. If success comes, fine, but that's not what it's about. In the spiritual life we must answer questions that have little to do with our cultural values. For this reason, it's hard to embrace the Good News. Doing so requires that we shift gears and leave behind much of what the world embraces. Thankfully, the only question that we need ever ask ourselves is, am I trying? Success, as Paul VI, points out, depends largely on factors that we have no control over. It is really the work of the Holy Spirit, and he *will* reward our efforts with success—not the success the world offers but real success. But we must let him do it in his own time and in his own way.

It is indeed difficult to be patient and "wait for the hour when God [makes] our dialogue effective." We do so by listening with our hearts to others, waiting for their invitation, and then responding to the best of our ability. And we must leave success in God's hands. The life of dialogue is a way of life, and as we grow in it, our horizons begin to expand until we find ourselves entering a new world, a world in which we are sensitive to everything around us. Our only option then is to embrace this totality in a life of love. And this life of love is nothing less than the fulfillment of the life of dialogue.

The deeper meaning of dialogue that we have been looking at resonates with existential phenomenology. According to this school of modern philosophy, the individual is radically him or herself only within the framework of personal relationships. "Being," therefore, means being open to another. Thinkers like Buber, Jaspers, and Camus maintain that human relationships are central to human existence. Process philosophy has also reached the same conclusion:

> The "I" becomes truly a personality when it is united with its "Thou," and the greater that union, the greater the personality. Outside the interpersonal union, we have an individual but not a person. Existence, self-hood, or individuality, and meaning are all therefore to be found in the context of union or process.[6]

6. E. R. Baltazar, "Teilhard de Chardin: A Philosophy of Procession," *New Theology* #2 (New York: Macmillan, 1965), 143.

Psychological research has tended to support this view. Carl Rogers maintained that the self is formed through the individual's interaction with his environment and with other people.[7] C. H. Patterson also echoes this thesis in his work: "The self is a product of social experience, the result of the behavior of others towards the individual. . . . The self develops out of social interaction, and the individual's self-concept is his own definition of his relationship to the world about him."[8] These scientists reaffirm what experience shows each of us, that it is in relationships that we encounter life's great satisfactions, as well as its central conflicts.

From these examples we see that dialogue occurs in interpersonal relationships. For it is this type of relationship which is "the response of one's whole being to the otherness of the other, that otherness that is comprehended only when I open myself to him in the present and in the concrete situation and respond to his need even when he himself is not aware that he is addressing me."[9] Martin Buber refers to dialogue as an "I–Thou" relationship, a relationship of openness and mutuality between one individual and another. If, for example, a friendship is characterized by directness and mutual concern, and is valued in itself and not as a means to an end, it is an I–Thou relationship. If, on the other hand, it is characterized by insincerity and possessiveness, and is valued only as a means to an end, it is an I–it relationship. If we return to our discussion of Aelred for a moment, we can say that what Aelred called "carnal and worldly" relationships fall into Buber's I–It category. Spiritual, soul-friendships, on the other hand, are I–Thou relationships.

It is important to recognize that genuine dialogue is found in presence, in mutual honesty and openness. It is encountered

7. Carl Rogers et al., *Client-Centered Therapy: Its Current Practice, Implications, and Theory* (Boston: Houghton Mifflin, 1951), 498.

8. C. H. Patterson, *Counseling and Psychotherapy: Theory and Practice* (New York: Harper & Row, 1959), 143.

9. Maurice Freidman from the introduction to *Between Man and Man* by Martin Buber (New York: Macmillan, 1965), xvii.

in conversation, silence, in a smile, a wink, or a thousand other ways. In true dialogue, which is nothing less than soul-friendship, we find ourselves accepted, affirmed, healed, forgiven, and loved. And in these feelings we are reconciled with ourselves, with one another, and with God. It is here in dialogue, in spiritual friendship, that each of us truly finds himself, his self-worth, and can risk being fully known. In entering into such relationships, we can shed our masks and start to be loved and accepted for who we are. The need to graduate to this level of unconditional love is so fundamental that it is quite possibly the most pressing and crucial task of our journey.

In attempting to live a life of dialogue we discover meaning, and infallibly receive that incredible gift, the gift of a soul friend. God did not create us to go through life without a soul friend and if we walk on the journey alone, it is because we have made a choice not to open ourselves to the risks and the vulnerability of loving another. As I look back on my journey there have been relationships that caused me great pain—anxiety, confusion, anger, and even bitterness—which often tempted me never to get involved again, never to open myself to love or friendship. Now, I can say from experience, that all the hurts, the betrayals of trust and the trials that we encounter on our journey are all washed away and disappear into the past when we finally receive the gift of a soul friend! The only thing that can prevent you from receiving the gift is when you give way to the feeling that it just isn't worth it—it's too difficult to be vulnerable, to be open, to be loving—and turn to walk down the path of anger, bitterness, and finally cynicism. When things come to this pass, you feel as though you've lost your way and there is no meaning in your life.

Love and true friendship fulfill us and make our lives meaningful. Unfortunately, when we don't have them, we all too often try to compensate with things like sex and material wealth. Needless to say, those of us who look for solace in such pleasures only wind up more disillusioned than we were to start. However, when you feel discouraged, it is important to remember that no matter what happens to you on your pilgrimage, you must always hope in and believe that God needs you to accomplish his work in you, to transform you into the fullness of being as his child. The only way that this will not come to pass is if you decide to quit! Remember, the journey is from birth to death, and whether it's a short or long one, you *always* have the capacity to face the challenge of loving and being loved. It is a great adventure and yet it is also filled with mystery. Occasionally, you may get a glimpse of the beauty of your journey. You'll see that what you experienced as non-meaning was the very point of opening you to a deeper and richer life. But you must never give up.

Paul VI says that "dialogue is, then, a method of accomplishing the apostolic mission; it is an example of the art of spiritual communication."[10] Another way of putting this would be to say that it is a method of living out the commandment to love one another. It is, as he says, an "art," and like all arts it requires commitment, discipline, and above all practice. You have to work at it. One of my nephews is a very talented pianist and for a long time his dream has been to become a concert pianist. He works at it, practicing for hours every day because he wants to perfect his art. In the same way, if you wish to develop the art of spiritual communication, to discover real intimacy and find the depth and richness that has been given to you, you must work hard and keep at it!

My experience is that many of us find ourselves on a merry go-round with a lot of other people. Round and round we go. We get so accustomed to the security of being with the crowd that when someone invites us off the merry-go-round it is exciting, and yet scary. If we accept the invitation and get off the merry-go-round, we experience a pull to go back almost as soon as we begin to walk away from it . Everyone we know is there and even though it is meaningless and boring, it has nevertheless become comfortable; we know the different horses

10. *Ecclesiam Suam,* 34.

and the landscape never changes. In leaving the crowd, on the other hand, we are forced to embrace the insecurity that is part of any pilgrimage. But we also get to walk through the valleys, climb the mountains, and experience life as an exciting adventure. Having said yes to the invitation there is the absolute necessity to let go. When we pull up our anchors and lift our sails, the Holy Spirit will fill them with a fresh breeze and reveal to us the beauty of the sea, the skies, and the stars—in short, the beauty of life itself. He will carry us through the storms we encounter and eventually we'll enter the harbor of eternal life. Then, and then alone, will you fully realize that God was with you on every step of your journey. Meanwhile, we need only keep working to develop the art of love and friendship.

Paul VI says that there are four major characteristics of this art and that when we have integrated each of them, "the union of truth and charity, of understanding and love is achieved."[11] The first characteristic is clearness, and he points out that "this fundamental requirement is enough to enlist our apostolic care to review every angle of our language to guarantee that it be understandable, acceptable, and well-chosen."[12] Language allows us to express our thoughts and feelings to others, and it can be verbal or nonverbal. Sensitivity to language is essential to the life of dialogue. Words are not always exact, and sometimes lose their meaning or have different meanings for different people. Differences in sex, age, and social or cultural background can impart different nuances to the same words.

This came home to me personally when my work for the Center for Human Development brought me to other countries and cultures. I remember a priest in England once asking me what time I wanted to be "knocked up." Well, I was kind of stunned by the question until I learned that what he really meant was, what time did I want to get up. Another time someone told me that he was dying for a "fag." Of course, in England

---

11. Ibid., 34.
12. Ibid., 34.

that means, "I'm dying for a cigarette." But it was news to me! On the other hand, when I used the term "knickers" to describe the pants that we wore when we were boys, it had a totally different meaning for the English, Scots, and Australians. For them, knickers are women's underwear! Words and phrases do have different meanings, and if we want to enter into dialogue with others, it's crucial that our words be "understandable, acceptable, and well-chosen."

Language can also be nonverbal, as when we express ourselves through touch. Here again we must take care that our meaning is clearly understood. If we don't, dialogue can begin to break down. I often refer to touch as a sacrament, in that it is an external sign of an inward reality, the love we have for one another. In order for this to be true we must "check in" with the people we're close to in order to make sure our touches are appropriate and their meaning is understood. Achieving clearness requires a radical commitment to honesty, especially in the area of touch.

It's important to ask others what touch means to them, and whether or not it is an appropriate vehicle of expression. If you're being honest, and not just trying to meet your own needs, then you'll be able to ask such questions as: What does this say to you? How do you feel? What does it mean to you? How does this affect you? Such questions help to ensure honesty in dialogue. As long as the other is also being honest with you, you can be quite sure that you'll find the proper way to express your feelings in a way that will enhance and deepen the relationship. Everyone needs to touch and be touched. It is one of the most powerful forces we have in communicating love. Interestingly, all the sacraments involve touch and scripture shows us that Christ, our model, was comfortable with touch.

I confess that on my own journey there was a period where I was scared to death of touch, because it called forth emotions and feelings, and sometimes sexual desires. I saw this as dangerous, and something that had to be at least controlled, if not killed! Of course, simply repressing such feelings is a good way to become neurotic, and can lead you down paths that are even more dangerous than touch. I, therefore, had to rediscover this power within me and find the way to use this gift and to be able to receive it from others. At times, it's been a mine field! You will, no doubt, make mistakes and they are meant to be learning experiences which slowly, but most assuredly will bring you to the point of being able to exercise the power of touch and to receive it with inner peace and tranquillity.

The second characteristic of dialogue is "its meekness, the virtue which Christ sets before us to be learned from him: 'Learn of Me because I am meek and humble of heart.' (Mt. 1:29) . . . the dialogue is not proud, it is not bitter, it is not offensive . . . it is not a command, it is not an imposition. It is peaceful; it avoids violent methods; it is patient; it is generous."[13] Paul VI is describing what we used to call the life of virtue. One can see that meekness requires mutual respect, and avoids anything such as what we call "pressure." People who have found great meaning in such movements as Marriage Encounter or Cursio can exert a good deal of pressure on others to get involved. That pressure can often have the effect of turning the other person off. When people do this, despite all their good intentions, there's a discernible lack of peace in their words and actions, the peace that is always a sign of the presence of the Spirit. I'm not saying we shouldn't encourage others to participate in the things that have enriched our own journeys. However, our approach must be patient, generous, and not a command or an imposition if it is to be an encounter in dialogue. I believe that, more often than not, you win "converts" by just being yourself and letting the beauty, power, peace, and meaning that you've found radiate. You'll attract others to want to find what you've found much more quickly than through pressure; there is always a right moment and one must wait for that moment to arise. When we do wait patiently and in a spirit of meekness, we will be enriched because our encounter will be truly dialogical.

---

13. Ibid., 34.

The third characteristic is trust. Here Paul VI states that: "trust promotes confidence and friendship: it binds hearts in mutual adherence to the Good (God) which excludes all self-seeking."[14] For me, this is an extremely profound insight into the problems of our time. If it is true that in our society today there are many who lack self-confidence, have not found true friendship, have turned to materialism and the use of drugs, alcohol, sex and other forms of compensation, then according to Paul VI's insight it is due to the fact that we have lost trust. One of the most serious problems arising from the work and research of the Center for Human Development with priests, religious, and laity is the loss of trust!

This phenomenon, the failure to trust, hit me in the early days of the Ministry to Priests Program. In one of those early retreats that I was giving to priests, a priest approached me and asked if he could see me in private. I said, "Sure, when would you like to see me?" He replied, "If I don't see you now, I'll never see you." Well, as you can imagine, I sensed the urgency and invited him to come to my room. When he sat down he poured out his life and there was certainly plenty of "manure"—the faults and failures that arise from the fact that we are wounded human beings—but I didn't hear anything that would have, in my estimation, warranted the urgency that he felt. So, I said to him, "Well, you've revealed a lot so far, but there must be something more serious for you to have said what you did—either I see you now, or never." "No, Vince," he said, "that's it, but I'll tell you, I've been carrying this for over eighteen years and there isn't a priest in this diocese that I'd ever dare to share it with." Needless to say, I was shocked and deeply moved.

Several weeks later I went to give a retreat in a different diocese. After registering and finding my room, I joined the other priests for a happy hour. I spent much of it talking to an older priest who had no more than a couple drinks before the bell rang announcing supper. There was an incline from the corridor

14. Ibid., 34.

to the dining room and the floors were well waxed and polished. I got into a line to pick up my meal, took a seat at one of the tables, and began to eat. The last person to enter the dining room was the old priest whom I'd been with during the happy hour, and as he came down the incline he slipped and fell. The other priests in the dining hall all laughed and gave him a round of applause as he got up and did a little jig.

I left the table and went over to him. By that time, he'd entered the cafeteria line and his back was turned to the others. I put my arm around him and asked him if he was O.K. When he turned to me there were tears flowing down his cheeks.

"You get hurt when you fell down?" I asked.

"No, Vince," he replied, "I'm fine, but I'm never coming back to one of these things for the rest of my life."

I said, "You don't mean that."

Then he told me that the only reason he had come was because he had heard about my work with priests in the United States and wanted to hear me, but that I didn't understand.

"You see, Vince, I have a problem with drinking and sometimes I have too much. But you were standing with me during happy hour and you know I only had two drinks. I slipped on the ramp, but I'm not drunk! But before the night is over it'll be all over the diocese that I was drunk on retreat, and before I get back to my parish it'll be all over the town that I was drunk on retreat. I can't take it any longer and I'm never coming back!"

Before I could say anything, the bishop of the diocese had come up and was standing on his other side. He had heard the whole conversation and told the old priest that he wasn't going to let him go until he promised to come back. He went on to tell him that if he were in trouble himself, he could go to the old priest because he would have compassion and understanding, and that he wasn't sure he would find that in the others. The old man took his glasses off and wiped his face. The bishop gave him a hug, and he finally smiled. I'll never forget either of these two incidents. I assure you, such experiences are not the sole property of priests.

Not long afterwards I returned to my monastery and one day I found myself sitting on the well on top of the hill, one of my favorite spots, pondering the text of Pope Paul and the experiences that I just shared with you. I began to meditate on the passage in Scripture where Christ invites us to be his friends and tells us what friendship involves. If we respond to his invitation, he tells us that we must share everything in friendship, that to love another is very serious business—we must be willing to lay down our life for our friend. As I meditated on this I also recalled that he told us when we are holding something against another we should leave the altar and go seek out that individual. He does not tell us to go find a priest, a bishop, or anyone, for that matter, other than the individual. He then says that if the encounter with the individual is not productive then we should return with a friend. Finally, when these two steps have failed we can, and only then, go to the community.

In the early church these injunctions were seen to be very important and an offense against them was considered a sin against the Holy Spirit—a deadly sin because it can destroy another and is like a cancer that attacks the whole mystical body of Christ, the church! From these early centuries on through till the thirteenth century we find a rich heritage concerning soul-friendship. It was considered a terrible vice to gossip about others. Even in the Old Testament we are told, "there may be reconciliation with your friend except in the case of upbraiding, reproach, pride, disclosing of secrets or a treacherous wound" (Sir. 22:27). And St. Aelred refers to gossip when he speaks of,

> the revelation of hidden things, that is of secrets, than which nothing is more base, nothing more detestable, leaving no love and no charm between friends, but filling all with the bitterness of indignation and sprinkling all with the venom of hatred and grief. Hence it is written: "He that discloses the secret of a friend loses his credit. . . . to disclose the secrets of a friend leaves no hope to an unhappy soul" (Sir. 27:17,24). For what is more unfortunate than the man who loses faith and languishes in despair? The last vice by which friendship is dissolved is

treacherous persecution, which is nothing other than secret detraction. A treacherous blow indeed, it is the death-dealing blow of the serpent and the asp. "If a serpent bite in silence," says Solomon, "he is no better who backbites secretly" (Eccles. 10:11). Therefore, should you discover anyone habituated to these vices, you ought to avoid him. . . . Let us renounce slander, the avenger of which is God.[15]

The words of Cardinal Newman also come to mind, who said that the reason for a lack of sanctity in his time was that people could no longer trust the secrets of their hearts to one another. And, in our own times the words of Paul VI articulate clearly and profoundly that it is trust that fosters self-confidence and friendship and that only in friendship are our hearts bound up in God, which in turn prevents all self-seeking. According to Christ, the true meaning of life is found only in true, spiritual friendship— love of one another! When you haven't found soul-friendship you find yourself in the midst of meaningless compensations like material wealth, sex, and alcohol.

I could relate story after story of people I've encountered over the years who were devastated by gossip. Many of us seem to accept our need for gossip as readily as we accept our need to breathe! But gossip poisons the atmosphere that is necessary for true friendship to flourish. Each of us can do something about it if we heed Christ's injunction. The next time someone comes to you with a story about another person, you would do well to ask them if they have first gone to that person. If they respond in the negative, then suggest that they do so, and if that doesn't work out offer to go with them. After a couple of times the word will get out that you don't tolerate gossip or rumors. If each of us were to take this kind of gospel stand we would put a serious dent in this insidious vice, if not kill it! If you have ever experienced this in your own journey then you know the pain, the hurt, and the heroic effort involved in getting up and putting your trust in another.

---

15. Aelred of Rievaulx, *On Spiritual Friendship,* trans. Mary Eugenia Laker, S.S.N.D. (Kalamazoo, Mich.: Cistercian Publications, 1977), 97.

I'm always amazed that what the mystics refer to as the simples faults and failings that flow from our woundedness, we consider the "big ones," and what they refer to as the deadly sins, we have come to consider to be the "little ones"! Participating in gossip and spreading stories, true or false, are sins against the Spirit and attack the mystical body of Christ: the individual member and the community.

St. James points out in a very vivid way how terrible gossip and rumors are when he says:

> Once we put a bit into the horse's mouth, to make it do what we want, we have the whole animal under our control. Or think of ships: no matter how big they are, even if a gale is driving them, the man at the helm can steer them anywhere he likes by controlling a tiny rudder. So is the tongue only a tiny part of the body, but it can proudly claim that it does great things. Think how small a flame can set fire to a huge forest; the tongue is a flame like that. Among all the parts of the body, the tongue is a whole wicked world in itself; it infects the whole body; catching fire itself from hell, it sets fire to the whole wheel of creation. Wild animals and birds, reptiles and fish can all be tamed by man, and often are; but nobody can tame the tongue—it is a pest that will not keep still, full of deadly poison. We use it to bless the Lord and Father, but we also use it to curse men who are made in God's image; the blessing and the curse come out of the same mouth. My brothers this must be wrong. (Jm 3:3–11)

> Brothers, do not slander one another. Anyone who slanders a brother, or condemns him, is speaking against the Law and condemning the Law. But if you condemn the Law, you have stopped keeping it and become a judge over it. There is only one lawgiver and he is the only judge and has the power to acquit or to sentence. Who are you to give a verdict on your neighbor? (Jm 4:11,12)

St. James sums these truths up when he states: "Nobody must imagine that he is religious while he still goes on deceiving himself and not keeping control over his tongue; anyone who does this has the wrong idea of religion." (James 1:26)

It is indeed a major challenge to embrace the necessary discipline to control our tongues and refuse to participate in gossip. But we must nevertheless meet this challenge, because gossip is, as I've already said, one of the most destructive things I've encountered. We all know the agony we experience when something we've shared or done, which we entrusted to another, has been betrayed. Whom do we then turn to in order to reveal our inner struggles? Who can we trust? The Christian community cries out for an end to the destructive force of gossip and rumors.

The fourth characteristic of dialogue is *prudence*. St. Thomas Aquinas tells us that prudence is the queen of all the virtues. It is fascinating to see how Paul VI uses it in the context of dialogue. He says that prudence, "esteems highly the psychological and moral circumstances of the listener (cf. Matthew 7:6), whether he be a child, uneducated, unprepared, deficient, hostile; prudence strives to learn the sensitivities of the hearer and requires that we adapt ourselves and the manner of presentation in a reasonable way lest we be displeasing and incomprehensible."[16] Dialogue thus requires that we adapt ourselves to the sensitivities of the other, that we pay attention to where they are and where they're coming from. And knowing the psychological and moral circumstances of others requires that we learn to listen to ourselves. I must first be tuned into myself, capable of listening to my own heart and in touch with my own thoughts and feelings. Then I can listen to the heart of another and adapt myself when necessary. Once again you can see how important self-knowledge is and why the mystics maintain that we must be grounded in humility.

In meditating on these four characteristics of the art of spiritual communication—clearness, meekness, trust, and prudence—one begins to wonder how to bring them into the mainstream of our daily lives. On this subject, Paul VI writes:

---

16. *Ecclesiam Suam,* 34.

> Many, indeed are the forms that dialogue of salvation can take. It adapts itself to the needs of a concrete situation, it chooses the appropriate means, it does not bind itself to ineffectual theories and does not cling to hard and fast forms when these have lost their power to speak to men and move them. The question is of great importance, for it concerns the relation of the Church's mission to the lives of men in a given time and place, in a given culture and social setting.[17]

Each of us is given a mission, that of announcing and spreading the Good News of Christ. We are all given the opportunity to touch the lives of those we come in contact with, and we can touch them for better or for worse. It all depends on whether we are willing to love one another, willing to open our hearts to the gift of true friendship, and willing to walk with one another as wounded pilgrims who need each other's support and encouragement.

In the introduction I noted that in our society most people seem to be in the stage of "role conformity and role expectation." They live out their lives, striving only to be what others expect them to be. The role they play might be mother, father, doctor, priest, corporate executive, and so on. Once you assume a position in society, you conceive some idea of what that means and entails. This is where you begin to play the role, and stop being true to yourself. You cease to live as an authentic human being.

Paul VI offers us an alternative to role playing when he says: "In the very act of trying to make ourselves pastors, fathers, and teachers . . . we must make ourselves brothers."[18] Therefore, if you assume any of these roles you must first be willing to be a brother or a sister. *You must be willing to be you!* Otherwise, your role will prevent you from entering into true dialogue with your brothers and sisters.

When I first reflected on the above, it brought to mind the research that was going on concerning integration, internalization, and assimilation of content in the classroom. The research

---

17. Ibid., 35.
18. Ibid., 35–36.

indicated that if I remain in the role of professor and the student remains in his or her role, then all we have is the transmission of facts, figures, and data. Integration and internalization become rare, and students tend to regurgitate what has been given to them. It is only when I'm willing to come from around the podium and be Vincent Dwyer, and the students are able to be themselves that we have the possibility of integration and internalization. Hence, the need to get out of the roles and to be ourselves. Let me illustrate this with a few stories that had an impact on my grasp of the importance of this. Perhaps one of them will resonate with your own experience.

Years ago I was giving the center's report to the diocese of Manchester, New Hampshire, which was taking part in our Ministry to Priests Program. During one of the breaks an old priest approached me and said, "You must be Kevin and Norma's boy!" I was stunned. I didn't know the priest and yet he seemed to know my parents. My parents had grown up in Nashua, New Hampshire, and it turned out that the priest had been a childhood friend to both of them. He took me aside and when we sat down he proceeded to tell me stories about my parents, especially my father. After each story he would ask, "Did he ever tell you that?" Of course, I replied in the negative. We were running out of time and he concluded by saying, "I know one story your father must have told you; the time when we were down at your grandfather's farm and we got into his home made beer and had too much—now he must have told you that one!" When I had to say no again, he commented on how sad it was that they had never told me any of those stories. I remember saying to him, "Father, it's not just sad, it's tragic that my parents were part of a culture that told them to stay in their roles and not share any of their human weakness with their kids."

Right after that I went home and while searching for something I opened an old sea chest and I found a packet of letters written to my mother when she was at Skidmore College. The packet had a bow on it, and since my mother had been dead for many years, I presumed on her permission to take a peak. The first letter I opened was a "love letter." It was fascinating, page after page, but when I got to the end it was signed, "love John!" I said to myself, "That's not the old man!" There were others and each one was signed by someone else, and I sat there and thought to myself, "Boy, Mom really got around!" It was a little naive, to say the least, to think that my mother never went out with anyone besides Dad, but I wished she'd been able to share that part of her life with me.

I believe that, if they had been able to share their own stories of their journeys and struggles, it would have invited me to share mine with them. I too began to play the role and shared only what they expected from me. Society and culture had prevented us from moving beyond the relationship of parent to son to become friends.

Another story is from one summer when I borrowed my brother's boat and went sailing around Cape Cod. With me was one of my nephews, a friend of his, and a priest friend of mine. We anchored at Provincetown the first night and after supper we were sitting up topside when my nephew started to share some pretty heavy things. I asked him if he had shared them with his father and he said no. Then I asked if he had told his mother, and again he said no. I asked him if it was because I was a priest that he felt so easy in telling me his ups and downs.

"Oh, no! All of us kids feel that we can talk to you about anything, because you have always told us about your own struggles; how you got kicked out of school and everything. And Gramp told us a lot of other stories about you. So we feel like we can tell you anything."

So I said, "Oh, and you don't think your parents would be able to understand what you're going through?"

"No, they wouldn't understand," he said.

I then proceeded to tell him some stories, especially about his father, my brother. After each story he'd say, "I don't believe that!"

"Well, when we get home, you ask your father," I replied.

After sailing to the Vineyard and Nantucket we returned home. During that time I had pretty much forgotten about our conversation in Provincetown. When we arrived home we were unloading the boat before taking it to the mooring, and my nephew began to tell his father the stories I'd told him about my brother's youth. Needless to say, I was in trouble! My brother said, "That's the problem with you priests, you don't know how hard it is to raise kids these days, and we don't need you telling them any stories!"

After bringing the boat to the mooring, I rowed back to the house where we were having a family get together. He came over to me and apologized. He told me he didn't want to lose his son, and found it difficult to understand how his son could embrace me, and share with me whatever he wanted. He missed that gift in their relationship and asked me to help him. I then quoted Paul VI and suggested that it might be time for him to become a "brother."

"I'm his father, not his brother," he replied.

I went on to encourage him to let go of the role of father, and to open himself to being a brother, a friend. This meant that he had to be open to sharing his own struggles with his son, so that his son could relate to him in a new way. I told him that it wasn't something that required him to sit down and tell him everything about his life, but that he needed to share his own story at the right moment, and that the dialogue would create its own rhythm.

Several months passed and he called me one evening to tell me he wasn't sure about my advice. He then told me that my nephew had come home one night and asked him if he wanted to hear a joke. My brother put down the newspaper and said, "Sure!" Well, his son proceeded to tell him an off-color joke.

He said to me, "Can you imagine what would have happened if we ever did that with Dad?"

"Oh, sure," I said, "I can hear him yelling, and asking us who we'd been hanging around with, and concluding by saying, 'You're grounded!'"

"Exactly," my brother said. "And I felt like he was on one side of me, telling me to put him in his place, and you were on the other side, telling me to be myself, to be a brother."

"Well," I said, "what did you do?"

"Well, it was funny, so I laughed," my brother replied.

"That's great."

"No it isn't! He went on to tell me another one, even worse than the first!" Indeed, it's risky trying to be a brother, a friend.

Later on my nephew went off to college, and during his first year he wrote me a letter telling me that he thought he might flunk out and felt that he had let me down, and his parents too. I called him, and told him that I didn't care whether he stayed there or not, but I did care, very much, that he knew that I loved him as he was, believed in him, and would do anything I could do to support and help him. I then asked him if he wanted me to talk to his father, and he said that he'd appreciate that very much.

I called my brother, who'd been aware of his son's difficulties. I suggested that it would be great if he would invite his son to lunch and share his own experience in his first year at college. There was dead silence at the other end, and I asked if he was still there. "Yes, I'm here," he said finally. In his first year at college, my brother had had some academic difficulties that forced him to change majors and suffer the wrath of my father.

He invited my nephew to have lunch in the executive dining room of his company. He told him that he and his mother felt the same way I did—that they loved him, just as he was. He then went on to tell him about his own difficulties in his first year at college, how he'd had to change majors, but that doing so had merely opened up new doors for him in an area that he eventually found success in. "So you see," he told his son, "things do work out and they will work out for you, because you're a great guy!" When they stood up at the end of lunch, my nephew hugged his father and thanked him. Upon returning to college, he wrote me a letter and told me that it was the first time that he had ever thought that he and his father could become friends!

Behold the incredible power and beauty that deeply touched both of them in and through sharing, which changed their relationship from one based on role playing to real friendship! Each of us has the opportunity to step aside from the roles we assume, or which others try to impose on us, and live a life of true dialogue, loving one another just as we are!

The life of dialogue, of true friendship and love, is the path to deep, inner meaning. It offers each of us a way of living out our commitment to follow Christ. It does require commitment. And like other commitments we must put everything into it if we ever hope to experience the fruit of our labors. When we only invest 95 percent, or even 99 percent, there remains a part of us that is not committed and that part will slowly eat away at what we're about, eventually destroying our commitment.

> It is a cause of joy and comfort to see that such a dialogue is already in existence in the Church and in the areas which surround it. The Church today is more than ever alive. But it seems good to consider that everything still remains to be done; the work begins today and never comes to an end. This is the law of our temporal, earthly pilgrimage.[19]

Thus, as Paul VI says, we must each take up the challenge of dialogue and begin anew each day, for it offers us the way of truly loving one another, of following the Lord!

The winds of God's grace are always blowing; we need only make the effort to lift our sails.

---

19. Ibid., 13.

5 THE LIFE OF A WOUNDED PILGRIM

To live a life of dialogue requires effort, perseverance, and a willingness to begin anew each day. This presupposes a deep commitment to a way of life. Dialogue, as we have discussed it, is the relationship that exists between an I and a Thou, and it also determines the communication that takes place between the two. The person who has opted for a life of dialogue has chosen a way that is open to all. No one is excluded! Martin Buber writes:

> The life of dialogue is no privilege of intellectual activity like dialectic. It does not begin in the upper story of humanity. It begins no higher than where humanity begins. There are no gifted and ungifted here, only those who give themselves and those who withhold themselves. And he who gives himself . . . does not know that he has it in himself . . . he will just find it, "and finding, be amazed."[1]

To enter dialogue, true friendship, one must be trying to be totally present, listening beyond words to the heart of another, being both a teacher and a learner, able to give and to receive love. Above all, one must be able to forgive and be forgiven, to heal and be healed in and though others. The dialogical life cannot be lived without a basic awareness that we have been created to relate, that only in loving one another do we find ultimate meaning.

---

1. Martin Buber, *Between Man and Man* (New York: Macmillan, 1965), 35.

As I've pointed out, dialogue is not mere conversation, it is much more. Its opposite is monologue, and Buber tells us that

> the "Eros of monologue" has many varieties: there a lover stamps around and is in love only with his passion. There one is enjoying his differentiated feelings like medal-ribbons. There one is enjoying the adventure of his own fascinating effect. There one is gazing enraptured at the spectacle of his own supposed surrender. There one is collecting excitement. There one is displaying his "power" . . . there one is delighting to exist simultaneously as himself and as an idol very unlike himself . . . and so on and on—all the manifold monologists with their mirrors, in the apartment of the most intimate dialogue! . . . They are all beating the air.[2]

On this same note, Paul Tournier writes that "the whole difference between an individual and a person is that the individual associates, whereas the person communicates."[3] The more you refuse to communicate, to enter into the life of relatedness that leads to soul-friendship, the more you sink into a monological world in which there is no meaning. The monological person is only concerned with himself. He or she refuses to respond as a whole person, and is only physically present to other people. Such people often lead others to make expectations of them that they're ultimately unwilling to meet. They manipulate others for the sole purpose of serving and confirming themselves. Here lies the closest thing to true sin, when we deal with others in terms of their usefulness for meeting our own needs, treating them as nothing more than objects. Buber articulates the depravity of ignoring another's humanity in this way when he writes that "love without dialogue, without real outgoing to the other, reaching to the other, and companying with the other, the love remaining with itself . . . this is called Lucifer."[4]

---

2. Ibid., 29–30.

3. Paul Tournier, *The Meaning of Persons* (New York: Harper & Row, 1957), 4–6.

4. Buber, *Between Man and Man,* 21.

Scripture tells us that we are created in the image and likeness of God, that we are born into original sin, and that we are wounded pilgrims on a journey to the Father who is love. Each of us is created to love and be loved, and the perfection of this love is the purpose of our lives. I must point out that perfection is also a gift, one we discover in trying to follow Christ, and trying to love one another. Perfection of virtue, of a chosen state of life, and for that matter, of any aspect of our lives is rarely, if ever, given or achieved in an instant—it is the work of a life time!

At birth we are totally dependent for all our needs, and one of our most important needs is being touched. Research has shown that frustrations of the need to be touched and cared for causes anxiety that can develop into psychosomatic disorders and other neuroses. Research has also shown that the first six years of our life are critical in establishing our ability to love and be loved. That's kind of scary! Very few of us were born into a family with perfect mothers and fathers, and within an environment that was ideal. We all struggle on our own journey, just as our parents did before us. There was only one person who was born perfect: Jesus Christ! The rest of us must face the fact that we have all kinds of needs. And sometimes we try to meet these needs in ways that are not borne from love, but rather from selfishness. So, we are all mixtures of both good and evil.

This is a fundamental human weakness that we had nothing to do with—it is a given. As *The Cloud* author reminds us, "we will never be entirely free in this life, no matter how holy we become."[5] And since this woundedness is a given, we must come to embrace it, accept it, and deal with it. You'll get yourself into a quagmire, however, if you fail to embrace another given: the unconditional love of God! His love embraces you just as you are—in all of your imperfections and sinfulness. He has revealed this incredible love in and through his Son, Jesus Christ, who became a human person, just like us except for that

---

5. William Johnston, ed. *The Cloud of Unknowing* (Garden City, N.Y.: Doubleday/Image Books, 1973), 65.

basic disorientation that we call original sin. This love was expressed in the fullest possible way when he died for each of us on the cross. He took upon himself all of our faults, failures, sins, and made them his own so that you and I could be free, free to live as children of God.

I have become convinced, from meditating on my own journey and walking with others, that the only significant crisis in life is failing to embrace the totality of the redemptive act of Christ in our own lives. He has already embraced us, even those very qualities that we so dislike about ourselves, all because of his all-embracing and unconditional love for each of us. This unconditional love is a given, but we are free to either accept or reject it. However, our lives are changed radically when we embrace and accept this gift.

None of us is perfect, and our journeys of necessity are littered with failures and sins. But eventually, we cry out from our hearts that we've fallen short of the way we wanted to live. To paraphrase St. Paul, we fail to carry out the things we want to do, and we find ourselves doing the things we hate. St. Paul describes this struggle between his desire to follow Christ and the reality of falling short of his goal as a direct result of "sin within me" (Romans 7:15–25). Our woundedness is indeed a given, and the struggle to love and be loved, to taste that unconditional love of God, is the work of a lifetime. But each of *is* destined to reach the peak of the mountain where everything comes together in the vision of his perfect love. That transformation into the fullness of the life of Christ requires our devotion and effort, but it is mainly the work of the Holy Spirit.

As human beings, from birth onward we reach out for affirmation, acceptance, and security. We long to know and be known, to love and be loved. There are many times on the journey that we fail; fail to be dialogical, fail in the bonds of love and friendship. And yet, these failures, and even our sins, are invitations to learn and grow. Although they are painful, they can become steps on the staircase to perfect union with God.

In the Christian tradition we are told over and over again that life is essentially a growth into the freedom and perfection of friendship, friendship with one another and with God. Aelred integrates these two ideals when he writes, "God is friendship and that one who dwells in friendship dwells in God and God in him."[6] Hence, friendship and love are the very foundations of the Christian life, and one's openness to and experience of them are what bring meaning and fulfillment. The refusal to give and receive love will inevitably bring death to the soul. The demands and the seriousness of love are again well expressed in a line from St. Exupery's *The Little Prince*: "When you tame someone, you become responsible forever." In other words, every time I communicate my love to another I have made a commitment, forever! I'm saying that I'll always try to respond to the other, with all that I am and have—without boundaries or limitations.

We live in a world where the word "love" is used pretty widely—in popular songs, movies, novels, plays, and so forth. This widespread use of the word is indicative of the hunger so many people feel for love and friendship, a need that we acquire at the moment of our birth. As we reach out to others to discover and experience love we will inevitably encounter the pain and self-doubt that arise when we're unable to "pull it off," or when others are unable to respond. There are relationships on the journey that began with the hope and dream of intimacy, friendship, and commitment, only to fall apart. Like the tide, the sea ebbs and we find ourselves on the sand, left behind, vulnerable and tempted to pull out, to quit. However, when you feel tempted in this way, you must pick yourself up, embrace your cross, and let Jesus help you. The mystics and saints encourage us in such situations to run to him, and in running to him with our hurts and failures we experience acceptance, forgiveness, and healing. The greatest difficulty is in taking that fist step of believing and trusting in him.

---

6. Aelred of Rievaulx, *On Spiritual Friendship*, trans. Mary Eugenia Laker, S.S.N.D. (Kalamazoo, Mich.: Cistercian Publications, 1977), 66.

The principles of dialogue and friendship must come into play in every relationship we enter. We first create an environment of invitation, leaving others free to accept or reject our invitation to relationship. When someone does respond, then we have the beginning of a process that can lead to the depths of intimacy and love. Every relationship begins with two people's desire to know each other and involves a mutual sharing that requires a listening heart. There is a flow that the Holy Spirit guides and it's essential to heed his directions and not simply give way to the dictates of our needs. When our need to know and be known become the driving force in a relationship, then we usually leave the flow, the rhythm of dialogue, and find ourselves high and dry; and then the relationship falls apart. When a relationship dissolves this way, we are often tempted to build a wall around ourselves, but we must never give in to this temptation.

Affirmation, acceptance, and love are offered to us in many ways, and it's important sometimes to reflect on all the positive elements of our journey. If we fail to do this, we will continue to suffer from poor self-image, poor self-concept. I'm continually amazed that some of my nieces and nephews identify their lack of a positive self-concept with the lack of affirmation, acceptance, and love on the part of their parents and the rest of us. However, when I've had the opportunity to talk about it with them, it always turns out that they've simply missed most of the positive things that happened on their journey. And so, they feel bad about themselves.

There was a popular song during World War II whose message I think we would all do well to put into practice: "You've got to accentuate the positive, eliminate the negative, latch on to the affirmative, don't mess with Mr. In-Between!" God is continually trying to communicate his unconditional love to us; the affirmation, acceptance, and love we so deeply desire, through the events of our journey, and especially through people. We often miss this tremendous gift, however, because we're too busy expecting it to come from a particular person from whom we'd especially like to receive it. Meanwhile, God has chosen to give it to us through another source, and we're missing the boat.

It sometimes happens that a relationship we're in begins to feel as though it's reached a plateau in its development. It doesn't offer us the depth and intimacy that we hunger for. But intimacy, you must remember, is a gift and cannot be forced! There are a lot of people today who try to produce intimacy at any cost, and no doubt, this reflects our society's obsession with having everything in an instant: fast food, crash courses, instant breakfast, and so forth. But if you try to whip up intimacy like an instant breakfast, you can be absolutely sure that you'll be going without any breakfast!

It takes great patience and prudence to allow others to open themselves to us. We must learn to honor their freedom to be themselves. Those relationships that never go beyond the aforementioned plateau are painful, and yet you can never be sure that at some point in time, the other will break through the plateau, and so it's important to be patient and wait. In that waiting period you must maintain an attitude of openness, warmth, and readiness to respond. In my own journey there have been relationships that took years to move to a new level; others seemed stalled or broken, only to be suddenly healed in a way that opened them once again to the flow and rhythm of dialogue. As in all aspects of the spiritual life, the trick is in never losing faith, never giving up.

Loving one another and being loved is a task that opens us to peak experiences and transcendence. But it's also extremely challenging, because love never stays on an intellectual level, but involves our emotions and passions, and can even call forth our sexual drives. In the old days we were often encouraged to "love intellectually." This insured that loving relationships would always be secure from failures or sin. The down side, of course, is that it can't mean very much to others when we tell them, "I'm in love with your intellect"! This kind of love is certainly safe, but it isn't real!

A relationship that calls us into the bonds of love and friendship naturally brings our emotions, and yes, even our passions, into play. This is simply a normal development. But in the past, most of us were taught to put strict controls on this area of our lives, if not to stifle it completely. We ran five miles, took cold showers, or did whatever was needed to kill this sudden flow of energy and power. This was simply the command we heard from our conscience, which had been shaped by the various "moral" authorities in our lives. Unfortunately, you can try whatever you like but you won't succeed in suppressing sexual feelings. For God created them so that we could learn to use them in a positive and constructive way within those relationships that call us to friendship and love.

The sexual drives and feelings that God has given us are a beautiful and powerful gift! Sex is not ugly or dirty, even though there are those who might see it that way. In loving relationships you will experience this area of your personhood being called forth, and it is indeed a great challenge to integrate that energy within the context of your chosen state of life. You can try to run from it by breaking off the relationships in which you experience this area of your self, but you can be sure that it will surface again and again. We must all face the need to become comfortable with our sexuality and realize that sexual expression is a beautiful gift. And yet, sex itself is not necessary for achieving intimacy or soul-friendship.

Our intellect, emotions, and sexuality are all gifts from God! There is absolutely nothing wrong with any of them. What is wrong, however, is when we use them to manipulate other people. Where there is no commitment, no dialogue, no real honesty—in short, when there is only you and the other whom you've turned into an object—this is where sin is. This is what sin is all about.

In the past, people were under the opinion that a person chose his or her sexual orientation and therefore was responsible for that orientation. We now know that this is false. Research has demonstrated that sexual identity is established in the first few years of life before we know anything about sex, let alone how to choose our orientation. Your sexual orientation doesn't make a bit of difference, at least not in God's eyes. What is important is that you learn to embrace that identity, be comfortable with it, and know that as important as sex might be, it is not essential to the intimacy which *is* essential to finding true meaning in your life. The same challenges in living out the principles of dialogue and the life of spiritual friendship must be faced whether your sexual orientation is heterosexual, homosexual, bisexual, or trisexual! (I always throw in the "trisexual" to make sure I've covered every possibility!)

We must all come to grips with our sexual identity; it is part of us and, ultimately, part of God's plan. If we are to live our lives as whole persons, there is no alternative. But sexuality and sexual expression are two different things. Once we accept our sexuality, and embrace it as our own, then we can begin to work with sexual expression in those relationships that involve us as total human persons. Today, there is a great deal of sexual expression which is little more than an attempt to satisfy one's own needs; the other person becomes an object, no more valuable than a lollipop or an ice cream cone. In these encounters, we see a destructive force that leaves broken human beings in its wake.

Once again, it needs to be stated that true meaning is found only in the intimacy of soul friendship. Sexual expression can be powerful, beautiful, and a sign of unity. Nevertheless, it isn't essential to achieving intimacy. This is verified over and over again in marriages where, for various reasons, two people are unable to express their love for each other sexually. Many married couples have shared with me that, when sexual expression was denied their relationship because of health problems, they nevertheless found other ways to express their intimacy, because they were soul-friends.

The more we open ourselves to love and soul-friendship, the greater the possibility of our total involvement in such relationships. Inevitably there arises in such relationships the desire to express our affection and care. But the expression of affection involves touch, and this can lead us to other forms of expression that may or may not be true expressions of spiritual friendship and love. We are dealing with a very powerful force. In order to find the proper expression of touch in each relationship, since no two relationships are the same, we must ask questions to insure that the touch is a true and acceptable expression of our feelings.

When touch is used in a sacramental way, as I said earlier, it produces fruit: inner peace, growth in self-acceptance, and a deeper awareness of one's loveableness and tranquillity. These are signs of the presence of the Holy Spirit. On the other hand, if we find that we really don't want to ask any questions involving the meaning of touch, and in the wake of touch we experience tension, anxiety, a loss of self-esteem and, above all, a lack of inner peace, then we can be sure that the touch is taking us down the wrong path and we're headed for disaster. I say disaster because every time we violate true love, we inflict injury, not only on the other, but also on ourselves. The personhood of both is diminished!

The power of affection, when coupled with touch, can put us on a roller coaster that takes us where we don't really want to go. This is why there are some people who have concluded that the way to deal with this force is to suppress it, kill it, lock it up and throw away the key! That might be safe, but it is, in reality, death. Touch is an important part of the art of spiritual communication, and therefore, we must work at it; we must learn to touch and be touched with honesty. The alternative is to withdraw into your safe little world where you won't make any mistakes, you won't love, you won't fail. Instead, you'll live in your pride, conceit, and self-centeredness, compensating in a million different ways that seem more acceptable, but nevertheless have the same devastating result, that life will pass by and you'll never have lived, because you wouldn't take the risk to love or be loved.

Indeed, it is risky to love. And yet, is there another way? What clichè or pious sayings can we find to justify not coming to grips with the tremendous power of love, of communicating that which we have received from God? He gave us this love not so that we could bury it, but rather to touch others and bring them to the knowledge and experience of this same infinite love.

It seems that the commandments and various moral teachings of the church are continually being placed before us, but the task at hand does not lie in simply restating them to ourselves and one another. The task we face, it seems to me, is to find ways of dealing with our failures and sins in a constructive way. We need to deal with the fact that we are wounded and we do fall down, failing to live out our ideals. Like the old adage, "There is many a slip between the cup and the lip," most of us slip up somewhere between our ideals and our life as it is concretely lived.

In the course of our journey, we all make commitments based on our ideals and values. But as we strive to live them out, even with the best of intentions, we sometimes fail. The gift of a vocation, whether it's marriage, the priesthood, religious life, or the single state is indeed a grace that moves us to accept the responsibilities of our vocation. One must never forget, though, that the fullness of the gift is rarely granted on the day that we respond to the call of our vocation. We do indeed receive the gift, but the perfection of the gift is God's work, and he gives it in his own time, and in his own way. Meanwhile, we must continuously strive to follow him and deal constructively with any failures we encounter on the road to soul-friendship and love.

The mystics and saints continually warn us against the sin of pride. Pride can be deeply rooted within us and in order to uproot this terrible sin and major obstacle to growth in the spiritual life we might have to fall, and even sin. However, in order to get at the roots of pride many of the spiritual authors write that God will allow us to fall in areas that we would most like to have complete control over. These lapses usually lead us to feel ashamed of ourselves. When you fall and your immediate reaction is "How could I ever have done that?" or, "What would other people think of me if they knew this?" you can be sure that the fault you've encountered is a direct attack on your *real* problem, which is pride!

On the other hand, if you were grounded in humility—as all the saints have been, and always will be—your reaction to failure would be: "What else is new? I can't make it on my own; I need to be forgiven and healed." And thus from failure, you would find yourself turning to God, either directly or indirectly, through another. Your woundedness would provide you the opportunity to seek forgiveness, and allow another to exercise the power we've all been given to forgive one another. Through that experience, you would taste the forgiveness, acceptance, and love of God. So you see, something far greater can happen when we embrace our failures, whatever they may be, and deal with them in a constructive way, rather than projecting them onto others or circumstances by saying, "He was being a jerk" or "I was drinking too much." When we say such things, we are only hoping to absolve ourselves of any responsibility for our actions.

Most of our faults and failures, especially in the areas of sexuality, alcohol, and overindulgence flow directly from our inherent woundedness. We can set out on every conceivable program to rid ourselves of them, but until we reach a point of seeing them as signs of something far more serious, we've missed the boat. As I've said, the far more serious problem we face is pride! Proud individuals do not reach out to seek forgiveness, nor are they filled with honest contrition and sorrow for any hurt they may have caused others through their failures. On the contrary, they spend their time in self-righteousness, assuming the role of judges of others' behavior. The wounded of this world will be saved; they will be forgiven and healed. Indeed, it is for their sake that Christ came into the world! But the proud and conceited walk a dangerous path, and only through faults and failures do they have the possibility of turning to God. So whatever, faults, failures, and sins you encounter on your journey, remember that you can rise from them. Learn from them, grow, and discover mercy, forgiveness, and the ability to love yourself as you are, in and through the friends you turn to, who provide you with a taste of the unconditional love of God.

I remember one evening when a woman whose family I've been especially close to called me. She was crying, and it took some time for her to tell me what the matter was, but eventually, she was able to share with me what was causing her so much pain. Her husband had just come home and confessed that he'd been having an affair. Her immediate reaction, arising from the pain and feelings of utter betrayal, was to leave him and get a divorce. During the conversation I asked her what she thought the revelation said to her, since he could have kept it a secret and never revealed it. After a pause, she said that he must have trusted her, trusted her love for him, and believed that somehow she would forgive him. I then asked her if she had ever experienced before, a situation or circumstance in which he had stood so completely naked before her, so in need of her understanding, compassion, and forgiveness? She admitted that he had never expressed such a radical need for her, and, in fact, had always been very self-assured and self-reliant. I asked her to consider that what had happened could well have been necessary for them to really enter the depths of soul-friendship, where they could share anything and know that the other would always be there.

In the end, she had the strength to forgive him, and their marriage was raised to a radically new level of communication, honesty, and mutual love and respect. I encouraged her to embrace him in his frailty, forgive him, and stressed to her how much he needed her. She returned home to him and did embrace him, in all of his weakness, and forgave him. Several years later, I was visiting the family, and she said, jokingly, "Well, Vince, I'm ready for him to have another affair!" When I asked her how come, she shared that the whole thing had set them on the path of true friendship, that they had never been so happy with each other. She concluded by saying, "Vince, this transcends any kind of honeymoon . . . we've become friends!"

Not all experiences of our woundedness end that way, but we do have the power, each one of us, to turn our failures into growth towards a deeper intimacy where we can stand naked and come to know that a friend can embrace us, just as we are! The things that we most dislike about ourselves, when known, *can* be accepted. Our beauty *and* our warts are what make us who we are, and whenever we experience another person loving us, as we are, it is a precious gift. That gift is a taste of his unconditional love for us, and it's an essential experience on the journey if we're going to continue climbing the mountain to soul-friendship!

When you become involved in relationships that evoke your capacity to love and be loved in return there's always the risk that you'll go beyond the proper limits and fail in your commitments. I have great compassion for people who are trying to love, and yet find they are unable to always and everywhere act in perfect accord with their values and the gospel teaching. Those who are trying to love and express that love may at times fall prey to their human frailty, and their need to be touched and held may well violate the dialogical process. But they're always capable of getting back on the right road.

I find it much easier to embrace those who are trying to love than those who are not. I recall a man who came to me once and shared that he slept with prostitutes on a fairly regular basis. He concluded by saying, "Well, you understand Father, it's only normal!" I had to tell him I didn't see anything "normal" about it at all, in fact I thought it was detestable to use another person as an object. I then asked him what he thought of people who went to gay bars to pick someone up? He exploded with all kinds of abusive language describing homosexuals. I said, "What's the difference? You use women and they use men." I went on to try and point out to him that all promiscuous behavior is deadly. He even tried to justify his behavior by saying, "But, Father, I tip well!" I just wanted to vomit! I don't think I'll ever be able to understand individuals who use others for their own pleasure with no love, and no commitment. When you try to reduce another person to the level of an object, that's sin.

As I've said before, almost all growth takes place as a result of mistakes. Yet, these mistakes can become a storehouse of

warning signals for the future, reminding us of the various pot-
holes and side roads that have deterred our progress in the past.
We all have the ability to learn from our mistakes and hopefully make new ones, rather than continuing to make the same
ones over and over again. However, in order to learn, one must
reflect, pray, and it can be very beneficial to share our journey
with a confidant, or soul-friend.

If we are having trouble with another person, and we feel
the need to confide our problem to someone, we must be very
careful not to reveal the name of the person in question. We
must always seek the permission of the other before revealing
his or her identity. Whatever has taken place between you and
another person is confidential, and any violation of that confidence is disastrous. Often, people will come to me and share
some difficulty that they're experiencing in a particular relationship, and before you know it, they've revealed who the
other person is. I immediately ask them if they have the permission of the other, and almost always they'll admit that they
don't. When I go on to ask them how they think the other person might feel if they knew that their identity had been
revealed, especially if I know the other person, they'll admit that
the other would probably be crushed. You can talk to me about
anything you choose, but you have no right to reveal, without
permission, the name of someone with whom you're having
difficulty. Everything that is shared and experienced in a relationship is sacred to that relationship.

I have known and directed many people on their spiritual
journey, and I assure you, tremendous pain and a terrible loss
of trust inevitably result when the confidences of a relationship
are betrayed. I now understand why Aelred maintained that this
fault was indeed the most wretched thing a Christian could do.
It is far more destructive than any lapse in the areas of sexuality, alcohol, or any of the other means by which we try to compensate for our human frailty and woundedness. Such betrayals
are deadly, because they crush the hope and trust within people, and attack the very life of a community. Paul VI pointed out

the consequences of the loss of trust in a relationship are poor self-concept, the loss of friendship, and a drifting into a life of materialistic compensations. One need only look at his own journey and the journey of others to see that this is so.

Some time ago, a priest friend called me to share a difficulty he was facing, which was quite serious. He eventually came to grips with what he had to do, and that involved getting some professional help to work through it. At that time, there were only three people with whom he had shared the problem and his subsequent decision to seek professional help. Shortly afterwards, I had to go to Rome for a meeting. While I was there, I ran into another priest from the same diocese, and he immediately asked if I knew that my friend had left the diocese for help. I asked him where he had heard that, and he told me that it was all over the diocese. It's impossible to find words adequate to describe the effects of gossip and rumors! As devastating as these effects are, gossip is a lot more common than any of us would want to believe, and not just with priests, but with everyone.

When I was growing up, there were things in the community that remained secret. People just seemed to understand that trust was sacred. This was especially true of any failings or problems in the family, the neighborhood, or, for that matter, in the local parish. We simply understood that it wasn't right to gossip about them, and you'd have a hard time finding any significant breaches of this confidence. Today, that sort of restraint seems to have vanished. There are people in this world who just can't wait to get to the nearest phone and blurt out the latest bit of "dirt" they've happened onto. I pray every day that we'll find our way to restoring an environment of trust and confidentiality in the world. And the shepherds of the church must challenge us to rebuild such an environment, because it is necessary for fostering the atmosphere of trust and love in which we can share, grow, and be healed. The plague of gossip and rumors is preventing people from growing into strong and healthy Christians.

As I look back, I realize that one of the great qualities of my father was that when you did something really bad and you expected the worst from him, that was when he said nothing! He seemed to be able to sense the shame and guilt that you felt and, for him, there wasn't any need to add to it. He must have sensed that you had already gotten the point, and it would be much more profitable to just let you get on with your life. I remember one time when I skipped school with some of my friends and we hitchhiked to Boston to go to the "Old Howard," a burlesque show. The odds must have been one in a million that my father would see us entering, but sure enough, he did. At the end of the show, we walked out to the street and there he was. I nearly fell through the sidewalk.

Dad, on the other hand, didn't miss a beat. "Oh," he said, "you boys had the day off? Do you want to go home with me?" He bought me and my friends train tickets, and talked with us as though nothing had happened. When we got off the train he offered everyone a ride home. As he dropped off each of my friends, I began to wonder what would happen to me when my last friend got out of the car and the two of us were alone. But when the last friend was gone, he still didn't say anything. So then I figured it would be after supper, or worse still, he would tell Mom and I'd get it from both of them. But he never said anything. Ever. It was over and forgotten. I can't recall my father ever reminding us of our past failings, especially the ones we felt ashamed of; for him they were finished. Needless to say, he did deliver a message in his silence. He was an incredible man, and at his funeral I told my family that I hoped each of us could live out our values as well as Dad did. I'm still trying.

Each of us is challenged to accept and embrace our woundedness, whatever it might be, and go on to grow into the fullness of the life of Christ. As I pointed out earlier, this woundedness is a given when we start the journey, not something we have chosen. This is indeed a profound mystery. Although the story of Adam and Eve attempts to explain it, there nevertheless remains the difficulty of understanding it, let alone accepting it. Our essential woundedness is an existential fact that no one escapes from. Scripture tells us that even the just man falls seven times in the day and yet rises up again (Proverbs 24:16). Christ said, "If your brother does something wrong, reprove him and, if he is sorry, forgive him. And if he wrongs you seven times a day and seven times comes back to you and says, 'I am sorry,' you must forgive him" (Luke 17:4). And when Peter asked Christ how many times we should forgive our brother, Christ responded by saying, "Not seven, I tell you, but seventy-seven times" (Matthew 18:22). It is because of this woundedness, and our need for forgiveness that Christ left us the sacrament of reconciliation.

In the life of dialogue, of friendship and love, there seems to be nothing quite so important as honesty. It has always been crucial, but it has become even more important in our time. In former times, for example, when someone entered marriage, the priesthood, or religious life everyone took for granted that it was forever. However, in our present culture such a radical stand is no longer taken for granted. Regardless of your own personal stand on the subject, most people have ceased to believe in hard and fast commitments.

Today, you rarely hear about the responsibilities that flow from our choices; for that matter, you rarely hear people speak of the "common good." There is an emphasis on the particular good, and that seems more and more to be determined by one's personal feelings. It's a sad state of affairs, and I fear for future generations. There seem to be fewer and fewer people who are willing to pay the price for their choices and, hence, the environmental factors so essential to a healthy society—the family, the community, and the church—are being progressively undermined.

I know that my parents didn't always have a smooth ride, and they may well have wondered at times if it was all worth it. However, in those days there were values in place, principles that supported them in their commitment and helped them to hang on and do the best they could. There was a deep sense of commitment that flowed from their free choice to enter marriage, and the same was true of the priesthood. I'm not saying that there aren't particular cases where a major choice involving commitment lacked the necessary freedom or that there couldn't be other circumstances that clearly indicated that the decision, the choice was wrong. Those things can and do happen, and it would be unfair to ask individuals in those situations to remain faithful to a commitment that had no real foundation. I merely want to stress the need for us to return to a proper sense of the "common good" for those who will follow us. There is always a need for models, and in this case, for people who will pay the price, to the best of their ability, to live out their commitments.

The present cultural situation requires each of us to exercise prudence and to strive for honesty. I can no longer, as a priest, take for granted that by simply wearing the clerical collar, I am indicating my internal commitment to everyone I meet. The same is true of the married person—the ring on your finger no longer tells others that you are "not available." This came home to me when I was a graduate student at Catholic University. The provincial of an order of nuns asked me to celebrate mass for their house of formation nearby, and to give some talks on the spiritual life. My first response was to explain that I was too busy, but she persisted and I finally agreed to do it. Eventually, I began to enjoy my weekly trips to the convent. It was my first experience of the awe that some people have around Trappist monks, and the young nuns seemed surprised to find me human. Still, whenever I spoke they hung on every word, as though there had to be some kind of mystical truth in anything that came from the mouth of a Trappist.

There were a number of very attractive young women in the group and I found myself enjoying their company, especially one in particular. We began to enjoy our time together and I became aware that I had strong feelings for her. It then became, for me, something like a ping-pong game, with the ball bouncing from one side of the net to the other. One side of me would say, "You have to deal with this in an honest way!" The other side would say, "What are you going to do if you tell her you have these feelings, and that you love her, and she thanks you but informs you she doesn't have the same feelings for you?" I sure didn't want to hear that! Then the second voice would say, "Besides, you're old enough to be her father!" But in response to that, on the other side of the net, I'd hear, "Hey, I may be losing my hair, but I'm still young and attractive."

I finally decided to be honest with her. We took a walk and I told her how I felt, and she confided that she felt the same way for me.

"Great!" I said. "Now we can talk about this."

"What do you want to talk about?" she asked.

"Well, you're a sister and I'm a monk and a priest—we need to talk about how to integrate all this into our commitments."

She then said, "I wasn't thinking about that—I was considering the possibility of us getting married." I was a little taken back, and had to tell her that I was committed to my vocation and that marriage wasn't a possibility for me. We did manage to talk it through, but after some time she left her community and got married.

This experience brought home to me in a powerful way how important it is to be honest in every relationship. When you aren't trying to be honest, you can lead others into thinking that you are a free person, free from previous commitments and responsibilities, and tremendous anguish and hurt can result. Love when coupled with touch, as I said earlier, requires a deep commitment to honesty. There is no escape from the obligation of raising questions in order to protect and support each dialogical relationship from becoming monological.

Each of us knows from our own lives that there are always "slips between the cup and the lip." However, it's also true that the only thing that can ever keep us from reaching our goal, perfect union with Christ, is the decision to quit. St. Paul reminds us that "all things work out unto good, for those who love." That incredible moment when all things do come together and actually work out unto good is the work of the Holy Spirit, and he will never fail us! The mystics assure us that we need to be confident that regardless of the temptations, faults, and failures we encounter, they can hinder us very little if we reach out to one another and to Christ for forgiveness. *The Cloud* author writes, "the remnants of original sin will plague you to the grave despite all your effort. . . . but never give up and do not become overly anxious about failing."[7] For a long time on my own journey I used to say, "It's too good to be true . . . it can't be true!" Now, I can say with my whole being, "It's too good to be true . . . but *true!*"

Once when I was a young monk, I went to see the old abbot, Dom Edmund Futterer, and told him I was discouraged at not making much headway in the spiritual life, and that I'd been feeling terrible about all my past failures. After listening to my story, he sent me off to look at a valuable tapestry that was located in the reception room of the monastery. He told me to observe the front and then the back side of the tapestry, and then return to him. When I came back, he asked me what I had observed. I described the beauty of the front to him, especially the detail and colors of the background. The back side, on the other hand, looked like a mess, a chaos of different colored threads.

Dom Edmund proceeded to tell me that life was something like that tapestry. The Holy Spirit was the weaver, and for the most part, we didn't get to see the beauty of his work; we saw only the back side of the tapestry. He then told me he would pray that one day I might get a peak at my own tapestry. Then I would see that if I eliminated from the work all that I didn't like about myself, all my faults and failures, I would in fact destroy the beauty—the front would be as ugly as the back. Many years passed before I was finally given a peak at the front side, and I was amazed at what the weaver had achieved. Recently, a person hearing this story gave me the following poem which I share with you. I have no idea who the author is; perhaps it was the person who gave it to me.

---

7. *The Cloud of Unknowing*, 90.

TAPESTRY

My life is but a weaving
Between my God and me.
He chooses all the colors
And weaves on merrily.

Sometimes he chooses dark hues.
And I, in blinded pride,
Forget he sees the upper
And I the under side.

Not till the looms are silent
And the shuttles cease to fly
Shall God unroll the fabric
And show the unknown why.

The dark hues are as useful
In the weaver's skillful hand
As the strands of gold and silver
In the pattern he has planned.

In one of the last letters Dom Edmund wrote, he summed it all up when he said: "Now I'm beginning [note this word] to realize that God has been in that poor, frustrated life all along; and it's a tremendous revelation of God's mercy. For so many years, I had seen but the underside, and the sight of my utter misery and frustration felt like a terrible weight bearing me down, while everything in my nature seemed to revolt and cry out: 'What's the use—cui bono?' Now, thank God, I see something of the upper side and my poor soul is amazed, for I see clearly that the spirit of God had been working all along, drawing straight with crooked lines." As long as we never quit, and continually seek to follow Christ, we will each reach a similar point on our journey as Dom Edmund. We will stand in awe of the power and beauty that God has created. And we will know that he does indeed draw straight with crooked lines.

It's important to realize that intimacy and depth in relationships are gifts; they are the work of the Holy Spirit in the unfolding process of a life of dialogue. One must let the dialogue follow its own course, in its own way, and in its own time towards depth and intimacy. There are many who think their hunger for intimacy can be appeased through sex, but as I've already pointed out, this is an illusion and leads not to true intimacy but to a loss of meaning. There are others who identify intimacy with "spilling one's guts." There are even workshops today where participants are encouraged to spill out their whole story. They "stand naked" before one another and affirm each other, thinking that this is intimacy. But this isn't intimacy; it is nothing but pure manipulation, a violation of the whole process of dialogue.

Once at a convention, a woman approached me and proceeded to pour out the story of her life. I thanked her for sharing with me, and assured her that God forgave her and that his love was unconditional. She then said, "I've just shared with you all of the secrets of my life—aren't you going to share yours?" I told her that I appreciated the confidence she had placed in me in sharing her secrets, but that I had no need nor a desire to share with her my own. She then asked me to at least share some personal detail of my life, to which I told her that I wouldn't share even one! You tell me a secret, and then I'll tell you one—this is not dialogue. On the contrary, it expresses a lurid curiosity that has nothing to do with intimacy. This type of revelation can be and almost always is manipulative and destructive to real intimacy.

We all need at least one person in our life to whom we can turn and share anything, someone we can be sure will remain steadfast, like the rock of Gibraltar, in communicating their unconditional love for us, just as we are! Each of us needs that person—a soul-friend! I continually remind the people in my life that they never have to reveal anything to me as long as they can always close their eyes and hear me asking them, "Hey, do you know what?" If they can hear me, they know in their hearts that I love them just as they are. However, if they ever were to reach a point when they might doubt that my love was steadfast, and that I could not accept them as they were, then, and only then, do they need to find me and reveal what they think could make me reject them.

This is what true friendship, soul-friendship, is all about. Intimacy and soul-friendship are borne from the rhythm of dialogue, guided by the work of the Holy Spirit. Outside the bonds of soul-friendship true intimacy doesn't exist, and all our attempts to arrive at it will lead only to disillusionment. At times, they can even lead to disaster. This is especially true when a person expects physical nakedness and sexual expression to bring it about. But while physical intimacy can be an expression of spiritual intimacy, it is more often than not, mere manipulation—using another person as an object.

As we proceed on our journey, it isn't long before we discover that our ideals, values, and yes, even our most solemn commitments are seldom perfectly realized. As we look at the life of the pilgrim, at his essential woundedness, perhaps you find yourself wondering, "So how do I move on? How do I deal, in some constructive way, with my woundedness?" I'm sure that, depending on who you pose those questions to, you'll get a variety of answers. Let me suggest three. They follow in sequence, with the third, in my opinion, being the most important.

The first is to open yourself to sharing with a soul friend. The desert fathers maintained that in merely surfacing the thoughts and problems that take away our inner peace, we receive the light we need to regain that inner peace. The Holy Spirit dwells within us. He is our spiritual director, and when we seek to deal with life situations, he helps us to face them in a positive and constructive way. Sharing with a true friend can create the necessary environment that provides us with insights, understandings, and the courage to face things.

The second approach is to seek professional help, someone who has the expertise to help us sort out the situation so that we can constructively deal with it. Such a person could be a competent spiritual director, a psychiatrist, or psychologist. Father Dominic Maruca, S.J., sets before us in very clear and precise language the aims and methods of these kinds of professional people:

CARING RELATIONSHIPS

	AIM	METHOD
GUIDANCE (Education)	To increase understanding and thereby enable a person to be an intelligent responsible agent in making an immediate decision.	Imparting knowledge or advice that is accurate and appropriate, historical and contemporary.
COUNSELING (Psychology)	To help a person increase his/her ability to relate in ways that satisfy his/her basic personality needs. To facilitate growth and minor adjustment through enhanced self-awareness and constructive changes in behavior.	Creating an empathetic relationship that assists to gain insight through constructive self-expression and objective clarification. Helping a client to see that living in self-contradictory ways violates one's sense of justice, integrity and respect for persons, and is a cause and not just a symptom of inner conflicts.
PSYCHOTHERAPY (Psychiatry)	To heal a person who is suffering from incapacitating distress due to unmet needs and deep conflicts.	Through the corrective emotional experience called transference, the patient experiences and expresses what he/she formerly experienced in reference to significant persons in his/her past life. The patient unconsciously transfers or projects onto the therapist; then these transferred wishes and feelings are analyzed and worked through.
SPIRITUAL DIRECTION	Gracefully to assist a fellow Christian in gaining a clearer understanding of commitment.	Through a continuous dialogical process of action and reflection, two pilgrims discuss God's invitation to more intimate communion with him, through an on-going companionship with his Son and Spirit in effecting growth.

There are times on the journey when each of us can benefit from seeking help through one of the resources described above. It is necessary at some point of our pilgrimage to do this in order to break the bonds that hold us down, so that we can regain our inner freedom and peace, and take our place as true children of God.

The third and most necessary element in our daily lives is prayer—spending time with God on each day of our journey. St. Teresa of Ávila points out that no matter how far you go in the life of prayer and union with God, you can still fall and that it is essential that you never stop spending time with God, day in and day out. All of the mystics and spiritual authors confirm this— without a regular prayer life you run a very dangerous course. Prayer allows us to step back from our daily preoccupations and hear the word of God in all kinds of ways. Prayer gives us the opportunity to look at our lives under the light of the Scriptures. It allows God to heal us, to give us strength, and to renew the power of the Holy Spirit in our daily lives. It is essential!

Prayer opens us to a way of handling our faults, failures, and sins in a constructive way. In the earlier days of my journey, I tended to pray only when I felt worthy of being in God's presence. I thought I was unworthy of being there when I didn't have things "put together," and so my prayer life seemed to consist of an endless series of beginnings. It was in the monastery that I came to a new understanding of prayer, and discovered I couldn't hope to follow him without it. There have been times when I felt tempted to give up that time with God for some other particular activity, but experience has taught me that I absolutely have to spend time with him each day. I won't say how much time one should spend in prayer, but some time each day is critical.

As you develop your prayer life you'll discover, if you haven't already, that it is all about relationship—your friendship with God. Prayer draws you into a growing awareness of the presence of the Friend who dwells within you. You'll find yourself reaching out to him in all kinds of situations, you'll confide in him and talk with him, as one with whom you can share anything. You'll also learn to listen to him. It is an experience that is most difficult to describe, but perhaps if you take a moment to reflect on a particular friendship that has enriched your life, and allowed you to share deeply, then multiply that by about a billion, you'll arrive at some idea of the intimacy that he offers each of us.

You need to come to a point where you can deal with God as a friend. One to whom you can turn to and just be. He is always present to us, hears us, and responds to us in so many different ways. As the author of *The Cloud of Unknowing* pointed out, the only other one that he needs is you. Without you, there can be no relationship, no friendship!

As you develop this relationship with him, you'll discover the ability to "let your hair down." When you feel lonely, yell out to him, ask him where he is, and tell him you need him. When you fall down, run to him and talk to him. "Hey, friend, where were you? You knew I was going to make a mess out of that situation, and look what happened. Next time, how about getting here a little earlier!" By running to him in every situation you'll discover that he will always embrace you and forgive you, and just like pure white snow falling on a city street and covering it in a blanket of beauty and peace, so too will he fold all of your cares in the abiding peace of his unconditional love.

When I was a child, we were taught that if there had never been original sin, there would be no wars, or any of the other burdens that we now carry. In other words, the world would have been a just and loving place to live in. They had a song in those day which was sung a great deal, especially during Lent, called "O Felix Culpa" (O Beautiful Fault). One day I was with my mom at the Lenten devotions in the afternoon after school, and they started to sing that song. I leaned over to mom and whispered, "Mom, why do they say that original sin was a beautiful fault?"

My mother replied, "Because through that fault Christ came!"

"But, Mom, the nuns say that if we didn't have original sin, we'd all be happy and there wouldn't be any of the problems we now have."

"But, we would never have known Christ!" she replied.

I thought about that for a moment and said, "I think that we would have been better off if he had stayed in heaven, and we were all happy!"

With that I received a stern look and a solid but loving rap on the head. "Don't ever say that again!"

We would all do well to gather up our sins and faults, sit down and write our own version of "O Beautiful Faults," because it is *through* them that we come to experience the unconditional love of God which, in fact, transcends all fault, all sin. Your faults provide an opportunity to reach out to your neighbor and to God, and through that reaching out, to receive forgiveness. There is nothing quite so fulfilling as when someone reaches out to you, and you have the power to listen, to be for them, to accept them, and even to forgive! One is always enriched through such encounters, and it is, to say the least, a very humbling experience. Remember, forgiveness is one of the greatest gifts of the Holy Spirit.

Our failures always raise our consciousness of the need for God and for one another. Our inherent weaknesses are the very source from which we draw the power of Christ, as St. Paul tell us. God is not about to give his power to anyone until he is absolutely sure that that person will never take credit for his gifts. This knowledge of our utter dependence upon him is the direct result of being in touch with our woundedness, and being in touch is related to the experience of failure. St. Teresa of Ávila insists that the first thing we must do in wanting to become whole, to be healed, is to accept and embrace ourselves as we are. Only when we have "accepted ownership" of ourselves can God begin the process of healing us and bringing us to wholeness. He will infallibly accomplish this, in his time and way—not ours! The only thing that can prevent this total transformation is quitting.

Let go of the past, let go of your sins. They have been for-given and he has embraced you, as you are. He has laid down his life for you. His love for you is unconditional! Spend time with him in prayer. Prayer will let you embrace the Good News and free you to be a child of God. Prayer is the source of integration; it is where the Holy Spirit teaches you how to follow Christ. In prayer you'll come to taste and know him, and you'll discover that he does hold you in the palm of his hand. He knows you by name, and he loves you without any conditions. He is not wait-ing for you to become perfect; he loves you, as you are! It's too good to be true, but true!

The winds of God's grace are always blowing; we need only make the effort to lift our sails.

6 THE LIFE OF PRAYER AND DISCIPLINE

THE PRECEDING CHAPTERS provide you with the means for building a foundation for your spiritual journey. We are now prepared to look at the essential ingredient of that journey: prayer. Although it is the most important aspect of your pilgrimage, it's also the one that poses the greatest difficulty for a lot of people. I have come to believe that this is mainly due to their view of what a life of prayer really is. This difficulty is compounded by the issue of discipline, which necessarily goes hand in hand with prayer. You might find it profitable to take a few moments and identify the people in your life who helped shape your view of prayer and discipline. What did they teach you?

In my early formation the two significant people who shaped my views were my mother and father. My father was very traditional in his approach to prayer; like most people of his generation, he thought that prayer was "doing something." You said your prayers! He had dozens of little novena booklets, and various devotions that helped him on his journey. And he always thought that when you prayed, you were supposed to kneel, and kneel straight up. When we prayed the rosary we all had to kneel, but my mother always sat in the most comfortable chair in the living room. Inevitably one of us would interrupt the prayer and ask if we could sit with Mom, because our knee caps hurt from kneeling.

His response would always be, "No! You should be kneeling when you pray!"

"But Dad, how come Mom gets to sit down and pray?"

The old man would turn to her and say, "You see, you're giving scandal to the kids; you should be on your knees when you pray!"

As always, she would look calmly at him and say, "You pray your way, and I'll pray mine."

If you spoke to my dad about a problem you were having, he would almost always go and fetch one of his novena booklets, and tell you to read it for the next seven days. But if Mom overheard him, she'd grab you as you passed through the kitchen and whisper, "Don't bother with his booklets, just go and spend some time quietly with God!" In those days, the custom was that you went to confession every Saturday night, and my father always made sure that we went, either in the afternoon or the evening. As I mentioned earlier, on one occasion we came out of the church after confession and my father asked my mother if she had confessed that she had not gone to mass on the preceding Sunday. She reminded him that some of the kids had been sick, and if there was any fault involved then it was God's fault that the kids got sick and she missed mass. My father thought that she should go back to the priest and check it out, but my mother told him that she had no problem in missing mass to take care of a child and that if he had a problem then he should go see the priest. Needless to say, it was a tense ride home that evening.

My father instilled in each of his kids a need for prayer. And he showed us how to pray using a variety of novenas and devotions that were popular in those days. Mass was central to his life and hardly a day went by when he didn't attend, sometimes at great sacrifice. His rosary and visits to the Blessed Sacrament were also very important to him. Above all he had a simple faith in God's Providence and would often say to us, "It's providential; it's all in God's plan!" Nevertheless, prayer for him involved doing something, mostly "saying your prayers." That was what he thought the spiritual life meant, and how he lived out his own journey.

My mother, on the other hand, approached prayer from a different point of view. For her, prayer was unique to each person, and doing or saying something wasn't really the point. The emphasis, for her, was on just being with God, not doing something, or reciting some words. Prayer was just spending quiet time with him. She once took me to the sea wall in Scituate and, as we sat there looking out on to the ocean, told me how important it was to learn how to listen to God in my life and spend time with him. She taught me to listen for his voice in the sea, in the wind, in the events and people who entered my life. She also explained how important it was to have places where I could go and just be with him. Finally, she told me that Christ was my closest friend and would always be with me; that he was inside of me and that I should be his good friend.

Both of my parents had their own approach to prayer, and their fidelity to their own views brought each of them very close to God. At the end of their journeys, they both radiated an inner peace and tranquillity; everything came together and they were ready to meet their God. The difficulty for me personally was that from the time Mom gave me her little conference on prayer, I never encountered any support for her approach until I entered the monastery. One's understanding of prayer is critical because the very expression of prayer flows from it, whether that means saying prayers, doing something, or just resting in his presence.

Prayer has been described in various ways, but it is always rooted in relationship, between God and the individual, and God and the community. It is an opening of the heart, an encounter with him. In each of these encounters, God reveals himself to us, he extends an invitation, and leaves us free to respond. This experience may occur in solitude, in community, in reading, in encounters with others, or in any one of a number of other ways. Our loving response to God's presence in any of these situations is prayer. On this note, Karl Rahner writes,

"The Commandment of Love is more than the fulfillment of the Law: it is also the essence of all true prayer."[1]

There have been, and still are, people who would like to restrict prayer to certain specific occasions or moments. Such people are not exceptional, but their position is hard to understand in light of the Scriptures. For Christ tells us that we ought to "pray continually and never lose heart" (Luke 18:1). And St. Paul repeatedly urges us to "pray at all times in the spirit" (Ephesians 6:18). The early monks endeavored to live out these injunctions by memorizing the Scriptures and repeating short passages as the they wove and unwove baskets. The history of the Jesus Prayer in Eastern spirituality points to the same desire for continual prayer. And there are a number of religious founders and foundresses who created spiritual exercises intended to help the individual to go forth to God in a spirit of encounter.

There would seem to be a contradiction for the Christian of our day who embraces the injunction to pray, but also has particular concerns and obligations in connection with his or her state in life, whether as mother, father, doctor, lawyer, laborer, or stock broker. Must we compartmentalize our lives and restrict prayer to one special area, or is it possible to integrate them?

As we look at the dialogical life, it becomes obvious that you can't live it without a commitment to prayer. In opting to follow Christ in a life of love, each of us chooses to develop and perfect the art of spiritual communication. Love is our supreme commandment and in loving we are united to God. "God is love and anyone who lives in love lives in God" (John 4:16). Rahner maintains that the love of God and love of neighbor are ontologically the same. In loving my neighbor, I am also loving God!

The life of dialogue requires that we meet each unfolding moment of reality in a spirit of openness. One cannot do this without love. If we accept that prayer is an encounter with God, then we must conclude that the dialogical person is praying by meeting each moment in a loving way. We can be doing

---

1. Karl Rahner, *On Prayer* (New York: Paulist Press, 1958), 34.

different things in any given moment: solitude, work, recreation, socializing, study, and so on. But in every situation, we are given the opportunity to meet the reality and responsibilities of the moment authentically through dialogue with God.

As the life of dialogue deepens, so does the life of prayer. It is impossible to comprehend the intimacy we share with the person we have never seen without first comprehending the intimacy we share with those we do see. We know that in those relationships that become true friendships we must undergo purifications, trials, and various kinds of difficulties as the process of call and response unfolds. But soul friends eventually arrive at a point in their relationship where they can communicate their commitment and love by way of signs and symbols. Such relationships, as Aelred pointed out, transcend themselves and infallibly lead into the presence of the person whom we have not seen, but by faith know is dwelling within each of us. St. Irenaeus once said that when two people love each other, it is God loving God. Scripture tells us time and again that the yardstick for our love for God is our love for one another. "He who does not love his brother whom he has seen, cannot love God whom he has not seen" (1 John 4:20).

It is indeed impossible for the dialogical person to avoid the invitation or refuse to respond to a personal dialogue with God. The response, in the past, has been identified, described, and named. You will, at times, find yourself reaching out to God and asking him to help you deal with certain situations in the context of his love. This is called the "prayer of petition." Other times, your heart will burst forth in gratitude to God. This is called the "prayer of thanksgiving." Sometimes, you will find yourself reading Scripture, reflecting and pondering his message. This is *lectio divina,* or spiritual reading. *Lectio divina* was traditionally viewed as a dialogue, an exchange of knowledge and love with God, and the Scriptures were the window to that exchange. Over the course of time, however, this knowledge and love has come to be drawn from beyond the Scriptures. Any book that speaks to the heart and spirit, any book that draws you closer to God can be used for *lectio* (even this one!). Our spiritual heritage should embrace all these different types of prayer.

St. Vincent de Paul once said to the Daughters of Charity that if they were called from the chapel to answer the door they should not think that they were leaving Christ, but simply meeting him in a new way. The "sacrament of the moment," popularized by the Jesuit, Jean-Pierre de Caussade, stresses that each moment is a sacrament in which God reveals himself. Usually, he does so in a hidden way, but he is nevertheless present. It takes great discipline to live in the "real world," where God is, and not create our own little world where it becomes impossible to find him. But we must nevertheless endeavor to meet the challenge. We must be prepared to meet, to respond, to encounter God in each changing moment, for this is what true prayer is all about!

Today, we take it for granted that everyone is unique, and, by extension, that every relationship is unique. It is clear, therefore, that we can only articulate the *principles* of prayer; each individual must face the task of internalizing them and expressing them according to the particulars of his or her journey. Indeed, it is impossible, if not plain crazy, to legislate methods for growing in the art of spiritual communication, for each person's method will be different. Each of us must come to grips with his or her own unique relationship with God. This is the only soil from which true prayer can grow.

At the very heart of the Christian message stands the bold assertion, "God is Love." The person of faith begins with John's pregnant affirmation, and allows it to lead where the Spirit wills. When we are so led, we begin to accept that we are made in the image and likeness of love. Love, then, is the alpha and omega of our very existence. Our Lord spoke of only one commandment as specifically his: "This is my commandment, that you love one another as I have loved you" (John 15:12). We have already said that the love of God and the love of one's friend grow simultaneously. When one grows, so does the other.

Everything and everyone, then, is an occasion for meeting God. The Christian is challenged to see life in terms of integration, not compartmentalization. True discipline is not withdrawal, but a radical openness to the people, tasks, and events we encounter from moment to moment. Thus, the Christian seizes each moment as an expression of the continuing incarnation of Christ. Martin Buber writes of the importance of the moment in *Between Man and Man*:

> I know no fullness but each mortal hour's fullness of claim and responsibility. Though far from being equal to it, yet I know that in the claim I am claimed and may respond in responsibility, and know who speaks and demands response. I do not know much more. If that is religion then it is just everything, simply all that is lived in its possibility of dialogue. [2]

On the same note, Hans Urs von Balthasar speaks of prayer as being something

> more than an exterior act performed out of a sense of duty, an act in which we tell God various things he already knows, a kind of daily attendance in the presence of the Sovereign who awaits, morning and evening, the submission of his subjects. . . . prayer is an exchange between God and the soul, and because in this exchange a definite language is used, obviously that of God himself, it can be looked upon as conversation. Prayer is a dialogue, not a monologue recited by men in God's presence.[3]

Since all knowledge and love of God is based on analogy, it becomes important to know and experience his love in those "visible" relationships that we have, in order to know something of the "invisible" relationship we have with him. Just as the life of love and friendship is an ongoing process of growth and development, so too is our friendship with God. It requires a constant effort and a perseverance that can come only from a deep personal commitment. Otherwise, one will drift from a life of love into a life of selfishness. As my good friend and colleague

---

2. Martin Buber, *Between Man and Man* (New York: Macmillan, 1965), 14.
3. Hans Urs von Balthasar, *Prayer* (New York: Paulist Press, 1961), 11.

Father Ernie Larkin, O.C. so often says, "Prayer is in life and comes out of life. Life is its matrix and proving ground!"

From my early childhood until I entered the monastery, I struggled to understand the life of prayer. There were times when prayer gave me consolation and deep inner peace, which made it easy for me to return for more periods. However, there were a great deal of in-between times when I did very little, if any, praying. Deep down, I felt the need and wanted it to make sense to me. Above all, I wanted prayer to become a part of me and not the result of a lot of "shoulds" and "oughts." As a young monk, the Holy Spirit opened my eyes and showed me what had been all along present in my heritage, but which I had never seen before. I came to this new understanding through the words of one of the early Fathers: "A training in prayer is a training in friendship."

The Center for Human Development's work with priests, religious, and laity has found two major problems in the prayer life of the individual: a loss of trust and a lack of consistency in the life of prayer. Too many people have lost the habit of spending time with God day in and day out, regardless of what happens. I believe that this problem in prayer is rooted in what I often refer to as a gap in our religious heritage; the teachings of the church fathers and our mystical tradition have been neglected for far too long and need to be surfaced for the people of our own time.

Sometimes, people quit praying each day because they have moved beyond their present form of prayer. Spiritually, they are ready for some new form, but they try to continue with the old. Eventually, they find themselves up against a wall. The way they are used to praying no longer has any meaning for them; it is no longer the proper means to express their relationship with God. But, without knowledge of how to continue the relationship in a new way, they can misinterpret their sense of loss and stop spending time with God altogether, in favor of at least making constructive use of their time by getting more involved in other areas of their lives.

If you maintain a prayer life that's anything less than a life of friendship, then you will almost certainly experience difficulty in remaining faithful to your time with the Lord, day in and day out, and, no doubt, will quit at some point. You may, perhaps, return to praying off and on due to feelings of guilt, through "shoulds" and "oughts." Only the framework of true friendship can help you remain constant. Even within that framework, however, one must realize that without discipline, perseverance, and faith, he will fall by the wayside.

The following diagram puts before you a way of looking at the development of true friendship and the name that we have traditionally given to each succeeding stage of growth in intimacy with the friend who dwells within us.

STAGES OF RELATIONSHIP—DEVELOPMENT OF FRIENDSHIP

STEPS	AIM	METHOD	PRAYER
Beginning	to develop a friendship	conversations concerning mutual interests	Vocal
Progressing	to know one another	an honest sharing of feelings and inner life	Meditation and Affective
Attainment	intimacy	spending time with one another, enjoying the beauty and love you've found	Contemplation

In the past there tended to be an emphasis on vocal prayer with few being encouraged to enter meditative and affective prayer, let alone contemplative prayer. In my estimation, this was due to a lack of understanding of our heritage. Even for those who entered the priesthood and religious life, contemplative prayer was not seen as a normal development in their prayer lives. Contemplative prayer was only for those who had been able to conquer all their faults and were "giants" in the life of virtue. Indeed, if you aspired to contemplative prayer, you needed to leave this terrible world we live in and join a special contemplative order. Only within the cloistered walls could one hope to receive this gift of contemplative prayer.

This view is, needless to say, pure heresy—every Christian is called to union with God, to intimacy and friendship with him. That's why we were created, and why Christ died for us. The old manuals on the spiritual life stress that contemplative prayer is a gift, but then go on to identify all the necessary dispositions we need in order to receive this "gift." It's as if God were dangling a carrot before us and saying that if we become perfect, he might give it to us. Crazy as all this seems, it's the viewpoint that many of us grew up with. However, the mystics and saints continually remind us that God longs to bring us to union with him. This union with him is a real gift; we don't *earn* it. God can bestow it anytime he desires. Still, most of us will receive it in and through our day-to-day struggle to follow him.

Vocal prayer is the usual starting point in the life of prayer. From there, many of us find that we want to know the Lord more deeply. That desire draws us into meditation, which is often described as a way of "getting to know the Lord." Traditionally, getting to know him was achieved by meditating on the Scriptures, which is a primary source of his self-revelation. However, it can happen that the Lord will invite you to draw even closer to the mystery of his being, and meditating on Scripture will no longer bring the consolation and peace that it formerly did. If, at this stage, you force yourself to continue this method, refusing to open yourself up and go beyond that stage, then the meditations that were once so powerful in inspiring you will begin to dry up. Once it dries up, you will become bored, and have to drag yourself to an encounter that no longer, seemingly, has any meaning; and then, you'll probably quit.

St. Teresa of Ávila, in describing the prayer life, uses the image of watering a garden. There is a well near the garden and you go there to fetch the water. You lower the bucket down the well and when it is full, you haul it up and then carry it to the garden. This is obviously hard work, but it's worth it since you're able to see the flowers begin to blossom and finally break forth in all their beauty. This is exactly what happens in the early stage of prayer. The work is very rewarding and you feel that you've accomplished something. Still, it's work.

But St. Teresa points out that there is another way of watering the garden which, while still involving some work, is nevertheless much easier and more productive. We can install a water wheel and an aqueduct which will carry the water to the garden. True, we still have to turn the wheel, but it is far less demanding then fetching the water with the bucket. This is analogous to what the soul does when it endeavors to be recollected in God's presence.

Or we can make things even easier. St. Teresa goes on to explain that we can move the garden near the river or stream, and then the water will just seep through the soil and take care of the garden. This is what happens when the Holy Spirit begins to take over our prayer life. Now it is time to set aside our own "work" and let him lead us. This is contemplative prayer.

Finally, Teresa explains that the garden can best be watered by the rain. This is the final goal of the prayer life— union with God!

Thus, when we start out on the life of prayer we don't mind the work; in fact, we enjoy it. We have the great feeling that *we* did something. Of course, there is a great deal of satisfaction and even a little pride in this achievement of ours. This is why God inevitably allows the water to dry up in the well, so that it becomes quite difficult to continue to go to the well when we know there isn't any water there. At this stage, we feel sad and frustrated as we watch the flowers we watered winter and die. But what he is trying to do in all of this is to get us to let go of all our little activities and ways of relating to him and just be with him, allowing the Holy Spirit to pray within us. This is difficult since we have lost the feeling of having done something.

The different flowers that I've discovered in the garden of my own journey have all been very special to me and sources of great help in praying and trying to love God. However, each of them eventually withered away, in spite of all my efforts to water it and care for it, trying to keep hold of the inspirations and insights that the flower once gave me. Each time it was as though God was saying, "Vincent, come with me, I want to show you the rest of the garden and all the other flowers," and I would reply, "Thanks for the invitation, but I'm not interested in any of the other flowers; I'd rather just stick with my rose." Therefore, he had no alternative in my case but to let the rose wither and die in order to get me to look at the other flowers. It took me a long time—and a lot of pain—to finally learn my lesson and let go.

Some of my "roses" over the years were Scripture, favorite spiritual authors, and various devotions. These were the means by which, at one time, he spoke to me and drew me closer to him. Today, however, I can only look back at them and give thanks for the day when they radiated beauty, light, and inspiration for me. Each one was a source of wonder, and helped to deepen my love for the Lord. But the time always came when I had to give them up and move on to something better.

It took me a long time to understand that the intimacy that God was calling me to had little, if anything, to do with me or my strengths and virtues, and everything to do with him and his unconditional love for me. He slowly taught me that he was the source of my strength, my comforter, and that his love, mercy, and compassion are all steadfast. He is always there and I need only put my total trust in him and spend time with him. My failures only make me more aware of my need for him, and thus always bring me immediately back to him. Scripture reminds us that he is a jealous God and is not about to give us his power until he has us in the palm of his hand, where we'll never take credit for the work he accomplishes in and through us. As *The Cloud* author points out, it is essential to be grounded in humility. Thus, the flaws that express our human frailty are meant to bring us ever deeper into humility, where we can enter into a greater intimacy with him.

We each carry different burdens, different crosses. St. Paul tried desperately to get the Lord to remove a particular weakness of his. But in the Lord's refusal to do so, Paul was able to realize that his power was not in his strength, but *in his weakness*. It was one of the few times that Paul remained silent, so that we are all invited to imagine that the weakness he struggled with is the very thing we struggle with. Hopefully, we too, will discover that our weaknesses are the source of our strength and power because of Christ. The mystics and saints are not telling us to sin, but they are telling us that we should turn to Christ in our weakness and, above all, remain faithful to a life of prayer. They assure us that in being faithful to prayer, "wasting time with the Master," we will be healed in his way and in his time. For he wants each of us to reach the fullness of union with him where we will discover integration and wholeness. Only infidelity to prayer can prevent that from taking place.

"Wasting time with the Master," was a popular saying in the early days, and needs to be rediscovered in an era that places too much emphasis on efficiency, time competency, and productivity. These concerns all undermine the value of just "wasting time" with God and with those who are close to us. In such a world, we can become too busy and lose a sense of the deeper meaning of our lives. We relegate to children the luxury of play and wasting time, and as each of us enters adulthood, it becomes nearly impossible to hold on to them.

This is a tremendous loss, because the person who has lost the ability to play has also lost the ability to pray. Leisure is crucial for fostering growth in both wisdom and friendship, and yet most of us seem to be putting it off for retirement. Its absence makes the call to intimacy in prayer and in friendship all the more difficult to heed. As a result, there are people in our society who believe that good works and a few short prayers are all that is needed for a spiritual life. Our tradition though, insists that wasting time with the Master on a daily basis is an absolute necessity. Without it, you'll find it difficult to meet each moment with the inner peace and beauty that invites others into dialogue and allows you to experience the Lord in a thousand different ways.

After Vatican II, there were priests, religious, and lay people who challenged and even laughed at many of the traditional devotions and ways of praying. They dispensed with them, and, in my estimation, failed to replace them, leaving people in a vacuum. People in the church who hungered for a spiritual life often found themselves lost and without direction. At that time, priests were trained for sacramental ministry and not for the role of spiritual leader and guide. Hence, they were ill equipped by their training to fill this vacuum.

Even today, many seminary programs lack the necessary formation in spirituality for young candidates to the priesthood. For me, it is shocking, when speaking to deacons concerning their training in ascetical and mystical theology, to discover they only had one course, or none at all. Most of them acknowledge that they have had no formal training in our mystical tradition. Patrology and spiritual theology have seemingly been deemed nonessential. Priests are rarely sent on for graduate work in the field of spirituality. Other fields are important, but the work of the Center for Human Development has found that there is a crying need for competently trained people to minister to the spiritual needs of the people of God.

This vacuum opened the doors to the East, where there were various masters and gurus bearing all kinds of goodies, which people flocked to discover. Transcendental Meditation became the "in thing." People who devoted two twenty-minute periods each day to this method were assured of lower blood pressure, inner tranquillity, and a release of their potential. Lay people, along with priests and religious, participated in these training programs as a way of filling the spiritual void they saw in the church.

During that time, I happened to be giving a speech in a particular diocese, and afterwards, a priest approached me while I was having a chat with the bishop, who had a reputation for being conservative. The priest asked me what I thought of TM, and the bishop started to walk away, but the priest asked him if he would return to listen to my response. I felt like I was being set up, and I asked the priest why he wanted to know. He then went on to tell the bishop and myself that the TM people had offered to come to his parish and give the TM training program to all the parishioners at a reduced price. In those days, the going rate was around $150 per person and they had offered him the bargain rate of only $100 for each couple in the parish. I asked him how many couples he had in his parish, and he said there were approximately a 1000.

"Gosh," I said, "that's a lot of money!" I then turned to the bishop and said, "Bishop, would you release Father for a few days so that we can teach him the method of Centering Prayer? Then, when he returns, we'll undercut the TM offer. He can then teach this old method in other parishes for fifty dollars a couple. Twenty-five dollars will stay in the parish and the other twenty-five dollars will go to the diocese."

It didn't take the bishop long to think that one over. "Father, when can you go?" he asked. And with that, the priest walked away.

TM can certainly help people, and it does foster recollection. However, it lacks the depth of a religious tradition and fails to nurture a life of friendship with the Lord who dwells within each of us. Our own tradition, on the other hand, is extremely rich in methods of prayer that help us become quiet and recollected, *and* draw us closer to Christ in friendship, which in turn brings us deep inner peace and tranquillity. In experiencing his peace, we find an ability to face the ups and downs of life. Prayer frees us from our enslavement to anxiety and establishes us in tranquillity. But the primary concern of prayer is not to lower your blood pressure or relax you; its sole purpose is to foster your growth in intimacy with the Lord. A fidelity to prayer in our tradition will certainly promote your physical and psychological well being, but these things flow from your union with God.

There is in our tradition what has been called the "prayer of quiet" or the "prayer of faith," and which today is being referred to as "Centering Prayer." TM was a response to a spiritual vacuum, and from that experience, many have been surprised to discover that all along, within our own tradition, there existed a method which could respond to their needs. To pray using this method, one must first take a comfortable position, which varies from person to person. You might find kneeling or sitting comfortably works best for you. On the other hand, you might find yourself in a hospital bed, unable to do either, and yet still be able to use the method. To start off with, I'd recommend you try sitting on an upright chair with your feet on the floor.

Begin by identifying a holy word or short phrase which you will use to foster your recollection and quiet time with the Lord. It will serve as a tool to bring you back to his presence when distractions come, and they will come. Perhaps you have a favorite passage in Scripture, the shorter the better, as the author of *The Cloud of Unknowing* tells us. Words and phrases such as *God, Jesus, Love, Have mercy on me*, or *Heal me* can be used. It is also very helpful if you can find a quiet place: at home, in a church, or some other place that offers you silence. Having taken your seat, close your eyes and begin to repeat the word or phrase gently to yourself. As you continue, you should begin to feel the presence of the friend who dwells within you. As that feeling grows, you can let go of the holy word. Just be silent and remain in his presence. If you find yourself distracted by thoughts, return to your word or phrase, repeating it slowly and gently until you are ready to go back to just being with him. You will find it difficult to be quiet at first, but slowly the Holy Spirit will teach you and you'll look forward to this quiet time with your friend. You should also discover that during various times of the day, you feel drawn to the source of your inner peace, to the friend who dwells within you. You'll have a new strength that will allow you to deal with others and daily events in a way that promotes the growth of all.

Some say that a person needs to do this for twenty to thirty minutes twice a day, or at least once a day. But I've met a lot of people who get discouraged when they can't persevere day in and day out with this sort of schedule. Things come up, and time seems to pass them by too quickly. They find that twenty or thirty minutes a day is more than they can take on, so they quit. If you are one of those people, let me offer you an easy alternative to quitting. If I can get you to just take *three minutes* twice a day, as a minimum of time with the Lord, I guarantee you that you will make great progress. Sometimes, the three minutes might expand to much more, but I must stress, the time you spend should *never be less* than three minutes twice a day. If you can do this much, it will become impossible for you to ever drift away from the Lord.

You will never abandon God in your life as long as you consistently rendezvous with him twice a day, putting yourself in his presence and just being with him; you cannot do this and at the same time be at odds with him. At the same time, you cannot pray in the above manner if you fall and fail to turn to him, saying, "I'm sorry." Only when you have asked him for forgiveness can you enter within and "waste time" with him. Fidelity to daily time in prayer is an absolute necessity, and we should all be able to find three minutes twice a day. Again, if you spend more, even a half hour, that's fine, but it should never be less than three minutes. If you can't even find three minutes twice a day to spend with the Lord, then you need to look at how you're living—something's out of whack!

For a long time, the rosary has been one of the most widely practiced means for entering into this quiet space with the Master. For people who've been saying it for a long time, it's an extremely effective way of becoming absorbed in his presence. These days, the rosary is considered passé by a lot of people— something that only old women pray, which is sad, because it can be an incredibly rich resource in one's prayer life. I remember one day when I was walking to the library at the University of Notre Dame, where the center's offices were located at the time. I was stopped by a student who had been waiting for me. I saw that he had a pair of beads in his hand, and asked him if he had been saying the rosary.

"Oh, no, Vince," he said, "these are Eastern worry beads, to help you quiet yourself. They're really terrific!" When he told me that he'd bought them at a steal for $2, I informed him that he could have picked up a rosary for much less. We went on to discuss the rosary and I discovered that he thought that the rosary meant saying a lot of Hail Marys. I explained to him that that was the way it was said, but people devoted to the rosary found that it brought them into the quiet presence of the Lord, and once absorbed in that presence, the beads were just a tool for staying there. I myself find it impossible to "say" the rosary, but I always keep it with me, and I so often find myself just holding it, moving from one bead to another . . . being drawn back into his presence!

Since prayer is rooted in life itself and takes its forms and expression from life, it is necessary to always be willing to let go of particular ways of praying. The Holy Spirit will guide and open each of us to ways of praying that respond to where we are on the journey. This is why you must never become wedded to one way of praying. As you grow in the relationship of friendship with the Lord, he will open you to new ways of being with him. But you must let his spirit lead you. When you close yourself off from his paths, which are infinitely varied and beautiful, and insist on doing things your way, you run a dangerous course, one where you'll inevitably find yourself saying, "I don't get anything out of it, so what's the use?" Then you will quit.

I can't overstress the importance of not quitting, and the need to be faithful to spending some time each day with the Lord. That fidelity makes all things possible, and in and through it you'll inevitably experience his presence within you and in your daily life. "Wasting time with the Lord" is one thing that you must make a priority if you want to find inner meaning on your journey. Without it, you'll drift, seek compensations, and that deep inner hunger for meaning will go unsatisfied. Daily prayer is essential, and some time must be spent in it. Even a few minutes are better than none at all!

Prayer is also found in community worship, especially in the sacramental life of the Christian. Father Edward Schillebeeckx, in his book *Christ the Sacrament of the Encounter with God,* writes that, "the sacraments bring about the encounter with Christ in exactly those seven instances in which, on account of the demands of special situations of Christian life, a man experiences a special and urgent need of communion with Him." He goes on to add that these special situations are "the divine act of redemption itself, manifest in the sacred environment of the living Church, making a concrete appeal to man and taking hold of him in a living way. . . . we can readily see that the sacraments are seen in the context of encounter, of interpersonal relationship."[4]

In the past, sacramental theology occupied itself with individual signs, the nature of their causality, and their *ex opere operato* efficacy, as well as with the minister and effects. However, today theology has shifted, and this has put the sacraments into a new perspective. This shift has been expressed in the following way:

> Christianity is not a doctrine, it is a person; it is not a theology, it is a history. "I preach Christ," says St. Paul, "and Christ crucified" (I Cor. 1:23). It centers on a unique act of divine self revelation; the Incarnation, life, death and resurrection of the second person of the Trinity. Man, strive as he might, could never attain the grace of union with the Godhead, so God in an act of supreme generosity willed to bring man to himself. This he could have done directly and immediately but he chose a way more consonant with the nature of his creature, the way of visible intervention, the way of sacrament. The sacrament provides personal encounter with God. In the sacraments God offers to men the invitation and means of coming to him, and man goes to God in a welcoming response. The sacrament is

---

4. Edward Schillebeeckx, *Christ the Sacrement of the Encounter with God* (New York: Sheed and Ward, 1963), 199.

the very condition of the dialogue between the God of heaven and the man of earth.[5]

The importance of the sacraments in the Christian life cannot be overemphasized. They are special moments that are prepared for in the spiritual and emotional maturity with which we approach the everyday acts of our lives. By the same token, they can be weakened when we lack fervor in our approach to these everyday acts. In short, the sacraments cannot be isolated from the everyday ups and downs of Christian life.

Since the sacraments offer the Christian a unique encounter with Christ, they are basic ingredients in his or her spiritual life. However, each individual must determine his or her own response to this invitation to ensure that it is a *real* encounter. The frequency of this response will vary from sacrament to sacrament, from person to person. For example, some people feel called to go to mass daily. For others, once a week is sufficient. We are called to witness to the incredible gift of the sacraments, but we must leave others free to respond to their invitation as they see fit.

At the same time, discipline is an essential aspect of prayer. Fidelity to a life of prayer without discipline is impossible. The life of discipline can be intense, but it must always flow from an interior freedom that opens us to the fullness of relationships—with one another, and with God. In opting for the Christian life, we enter an ongoing process, the lifelong commitment to the discipline that we need to keep our feet set firmly on the path that leads to his love, his freedom.

Like other key areas of the spiritual life that we have been considering, our perception of the life of discipline is very important. In the past many of us looked upon certain acts of discipline, such as fasting, mortification, and self-denial, as quite negative. During Advent and Lent there was a special emphasis

---

5. Denis O'Callaghan, ed., *Christ, Sacrament of God* (New York: Sheed and Ward, 1964), 43.

on giving up certain things that we enjoyed: sweets, smoking, drinking, and the like. This practice had as its goal the internalization of the need for self-denial. There were, in fact, rules governing these areas of our life. Paul VI, however, believing that it was safe to assume that all of us had indeed internalized the principle of discipline which is so necessary to the Christian life, removed many of these laws and rules. Once they were replaced with "guidelines," out went fasting, mortification, and self-denial. It was like having a great weight taken off our shoulders.

For the mystics, discipline was not negative, but a way to open us to freedom, the freedom to truly be, to love and to be loved. The various acts of discipline were merely tools that helped us to attain this freedom. If I say to you that I'm just a social drinker and can stop anytime I want, but never indeed stop drinking, then I might well be kidding myself—I might be hooked. The same could be said of smoking or, for that matter, anything that we use or experience on the journey. We like to think that freedom is easy, but in fact, it requires tremendous self-awareness to be completely free. Thus, for the mystics, discipline was a positive action taken in order to insure that they were truly free.

Earlier I referred to the human potential movement's research showing that one of the reasons that many of us fail to use more than 8 to 16 percent of our potential is due to poor physical fitness. If you believe what Christ tells us, that one day each of us will have to render an account for our gifts, then perhaps you'll feel challenged by this finding. If we were to find three persons, all living in more or less the same environment, doing the same type of work, and in different physical condition you'd see the contrast in a dramatic way. Let's take the first person who happens to be overweight and pays no attention to nutrition or exercise. The second is one of those people who never gain any weight, but nevertheless pay little, if any, attention to nutrition or exercise. The third person maintains proper weight, follows a balanced nutritional diet, and exercises; he is in good physical condition. Research shows that the first two use 80 percent of their energy to get through the day, while the third person uses only 20 percent of his energy, a 60 percent differential. Can the Christian afford to dissipate 60 percent of his or her energy each day, energy that is essential to living a life of love and friendship?

Yes, we have done away with fasting, mortification, and self-denial. But we have replaced them with proper weight, nutrition, and physical fitness. St. Paul describes the journey in terms of running a race. We all know what kind of shape you have to be in to run a race. If God were to come down and line us up for the start of the race, with the finish line bringing us eternal life, I'm not sure how many of us would make it to the finish line—even if it were only a hundred-yard dash! Call it by any name you like, the fact that this area of discipline requires constant effort is indisputable. When you lack the energy that flows from good physical fitness, then when you get home you can only make it to your comfortable chair, pour yourself a drink, and turn on the television. Of course, the television has to have a remote so that you don't have to get up and change the channels—that would take too much energy.

When we come in contact with the God of Revelation, and respond to his invitation to relationship we enter into a dynamic relationship with important responsibilities. Our "yes" to God's invitation initiates each of us into the process of being "clothed in Christ" (Galatians 3:27). This process necessarily involves us in a life of discipline. There are many types of discipline, and I won't attempt to give their history, but will confine myself to describing what Christian discipline has come to mean in our day. Our Lord says: "If any man wishes to come after me, let him deny himself and take up his cross and follow me. For whoever would save his life will lose it; and whosoever loses his life for my sake, and for the sake of the gospel, will save it" (Mark. 8:34–35). The Christian practices asceticism in order to freely confront this aspect of the Good News; it is the means by which he or she embraces the sacrifice to which Christ calls us. On this point Karl Rahner writes, "It is Christian asceticism when a man verifies that his preparedness for death is existentially serious and inwardly genuine by freely laying hold upon something of the passion of death above and beyond that which destiny itself imposes on him."[6] And elsewhere Rahner says, "Christian asceticism, understood as an existential yes to the God of supernatural life, is therefore a yes to Jesus Christ in particular . . . a yes to that mode of appearance of grace in the world which unveiled itself directly for the first time in the fate of Jesus, leading him to the Cross and death."[7]

The fact that we have a deeper understanding of ourselves than in the past means that we have, through the work of the Holy Spirit, been given new insights into our relationship with God, with one another, and with our environment. Discipline, then, may be looked upon in the light of this relational dimension as a means of creating an environment that will foster growth and deepen our relationships.

> A healthy asceticism does not proceed out of mistrust or contempt for the body, on the one hand, or for feeling and emotion, on the other. It is not a process to facilitate repression by serving as a defense against unacceptable feelings. It is a training procedure or therapy. The motives from which it proceeds should be healthy. It is the mature act of an adult who, for religious motives, renounces his personal impulses and desires; this renunciation he has accepted and healthily integrated into his life.[8]

From this you can see that discipline is a means, a tool, for living out one's commitment to follow Christ. Discipline enables the Christian to fulfill the commandment of love and to die to all that is or can become an obstacle to fulfilling that commandment. And it is the work of a lifetime. Without a

---

6. "Asceticism" from *Theological Dictionary*, ed. Cornelia Ernst, O.P., trans. Richard Strachan (New York: Herder & Herder, 1965), 38.

7. Karl Rahner, *Theological Investigations*, vol. 3 (Baltimore: Helicon, 1967) 81–82.

8. *New Catholic Encyclopedia*, vol. 1 (Washington, D.C.: Catholic University of America, 1967), 942.

definite commitment to discipline there can be no true living for others, let alone for God.

The person who chooses to follow Christ in the dialogical life has also chosen a life of discipline. One need only look at some of the aspects of what is required in dialogical living to realize that without discipline it cannot become a reality. Dialogue is an orientation, a radical disposition which attempts to meet each moment in openness and love. It is both the relationship between persons and the very principle that determines the nature of their exchange. The dialogical person communicates with the people and things around him or herself, and is open to receiving their communication. In *The Miracle of Dialogue,* Ruel Howe presents the characteristics the that are demanded of the person who chooses to live the life of dialogue:

> 1. The dialogical person is a total, authentic person. One responds to another with one's whole being—totally present to the other—one wears no "masks."

> 2. The dialogical person is an open person. One is free or willing to reveal oneself to another—able also to receive the revelation of another.

> 3. The dialogical person is a disciplined person. One employs whatever types of discipline that are necessary in promoting the growth and development of relationships.

> 4. The dialogical person is a related person. One realizes one's dependence upon others, and as one responds to them, one is being a responsible person—this takes tremendous courage.[9]

These characteristics of the dialogical person embrace all that can be said concerning the life of virtue, yet, they are framed in language that has meaning for those trying to lead spiritual lives in the world today. Furthermore, Howe's

---

9. Ruel Howe, *The Miracle of Dialogue* (New York: Seabury Press, 1963), 70–83.

approach stresses the interior aspect of virtue, whereas in the past, for many, the stress was on external actions.

We all experience the pulls between what we want to do, having chosen to follow Christ, and the non-loving actions that we sometimes find ourselves involved in. It is this very struggle that calls us to embrace discipline. Having chosen to follow Christ, and live his commandment of love, we must exercise discipline if we wish to remain faithful to a life of love, rather than give way to selfishness and various forms of manipulation and compensation.

As Karl Rahner points out there is no "recipe for the Christian life in practice, a single recipe for telling with absolute and eternal validity what must be the special gift of each individual."[10] The life of discipline will of necessity vary from person to person, and from moment to moment. However, without discipline there can be no true friendship, no authentic encounter with others, let alone with God. When there is no discipline one drifts along until, one day, he finally wakes up to find himself in the midst of utter loneliness and the total loss of meaning.

Our mystical tradition states clearly that in all things, except in love, we must practice moderation, or discipline. We also find an emphasis on a holistic approach that draws on our whole being. I've often felt that the mystics would have been very popular with a number of governments today, since they arrived at their insights about life without any grants to study the problem. For example, the author of *The Cloud of Unknowing* stresses the necessity of good health. He writes, "I am serious when I say that this work demands a relaxed, healthy, and vigorous disposition of both body and spirit. For the love of God, discipline yourself in body and spirit so that you preserve your health as long as you can." And he adds, "avoid illness as much as possible so that you are not responsible for unnecessary infirmity."[11] Even in the fourteenth century

---

10. Karl Rahner, *Theological Investigations,* vol. 3, 84–85.
11. *The Cloud of Unknowing,* 101.

the Christian was encouraged to stay in good physical condition so that the energy that flows from good health would be available to living a life of love.

There can be no doubt that the care of our physical well being is an essential element in the life of discipline. In the Center for Human Development's ministry programs it has been well established that those in ministry who are in good shape find that it enriches their ministry. But too many people fail to make this connection between physical well being and the spiritual life. In an age when health clubs, running and other forms of exercise have become quite popular, people need to know how important physical fitness is to following Christ and living out his commandment of love. The increased availability of energy, along with the sense of wellness that results from being in shape, fosters discipline in every aspect of our lives.

Even industries today are concerned about the good health of their employees. They are investing resources to offer physical fitness programs designed to improve health as well as provide recreation. One reason for this phenomenon indicated in research is that hundreds of millions of dollars are lost every year to replacing employees who wind up in hospital coronary wards—or morgues. And that's not to mention the staggering cost of sick leave, which is estimated to be well in excess of twenty billion dollars each year. Sixty percent of the people who exercise three times a week report having lost weight, and eighty-nine percent report improved stamina and greater ease in doing their work. Just as a daily commitment to prayer is essential, so too must we be committed to the discipline of maintaining our physical well being. Without such discipline, prayer will inevitably fall by the wayside.

Pope John Paul II, in his recent encyclical dealing with the Holy Spirit in the life of the church and the world unfolds for us a rich understanding of prayer and its power in our lives.

> The Holy Spirit is the gift that comes into man's heart together with prayer. In prayer he manifests himself first of all and

above all as the gift that "helps us in our weakness." This is the magnificent thought developed by Saint Paul in the letter to the Romans, when he writes: "For we do not know how to pray as we ought, but the Spirit himself intercedes for us with sights too deep for words." Therefore, the Holy Spirit not only enables us to pray, but guides us "from within" in prayer; he is present in our prayer and gives divine dimension. Thus "he who searches the hearts of men knows what is the mind of the Spirit, because the Spirit intercedes for the saints according to the will of God." Prayer through the power of the Holy Spirit becomes the ever more mature expression of the new man, who by means of this prayer participates in the divine life.[12]

The life of prayer and discipline is indeed challenging and demanding, and yet is there any other way? The journey will have its ups and downs, but as long as you never quit, the Holy Spirit will guide you, heal, support, and comfort you on your pilgrimage. As *The Cloud* author says, "the only other one He needs is you."

The winds of God's grace are always blowing; we need only make the effort to lift our sails.

12. Pope John Paul II, *The Lord and Giver of Life* (Washington, D.C.: United States Catholic Conference, 1986), 131–32.

CONCLUSION

Pope John Paul II has announced, in his recent encyclical on the Holy Spirit, that the church would celebrate a Jubilee of the year 2000 to mark the end of the twentieth century and the beginning of the third millennium since the birth of Christ. He writes:

> The great Jubilee to be celebrated at the end of this Millennium and at the beginning of the next ought to constitute a powerful call to all those who "worship God in spirit and truth." It should be for everyone a special occasion for meditating on the mystery of the Triune God, who in himself is wholly transcendent with regard to the world, especially the visible world. For he is absolute Spirit, "God is spirit"; and also, in such a marvelous way, he is not only close to this world but present in it, and in a sense immanent, penetrating it and giving it life from within. This is especially true in relation to man: God is present in the intimacy of man's being, in his mind, conscience and heart: an ontological and psychological reality, in considering which Saint Augustine said of God that he was "closer than my inmost being." These words help us to understand better the words of Jesus to the Samaritan woman: "God is spirit." Only the Spirit can be so immanent in man and in the world, while remaining inviolable and immutable in his absolute transcendence.

> But in Jesus Christ the divine presence in the world and in man has been made manifest in a new way and in visible form. In him "the grace of God has appeared indeed." The love of God the Father, as a gift, infinite grace, source of life, has been made visible in Christ, and in his humanity that love has become "part" of the universe, the human family and history. This

appearing grace in human history, through Jesus Christ, has accomplished through the poser of the Holy Spirit, who is the source of all God's salvific activity in the world: he, the "hidden God," who as love and gift "fills the universe." The Church's entire life, as will appear in the great Jubilee, means going to meet the invisible God, the hidden God: a meeting with the Spirit "who gives life."[1]

It is my own prayer that the preparation for this Jubilee will foster a reawakening of our great spiritual heritage. That it will indeed be a time when great efforts will be made to make known this heritage which embraces not only the sacred Scriptures, but also the writings of the Fathers and those great men and women who have formed and shaped our mystical tradition. The hunger of our day, and surely of the years ahead as we prepare to celebrate the beginning of a new millennium, is a hunger to experience God and live out our Christian commitment in a meaningful way. And we must not forget that we are indeed wounded pilgrims on a journey to the Father.

When I left on my sabbatical I wanted to find a place to hide, where I could study, reflect, and pray. In addition to that I was seeking an environment that would foster the writing and completion of this book. I settled eventually in Florence, Italy. A priest friend and I rented an apartment, a fourteenth-century tower in the center of the city. There were ninety-one steps to the entrance which provided us a serious workout every day. We named the tower, fittingly, "the Hermitage." It had four levels and the spiral staircase that led to the very top was another forty steps. At the top was a room filled with plants and flowers and it provided a panoramic view of the whole city of Florence. It was breathtaking! This is where I would go to reflect and pray.

Often, as I looked out on Florence, I reflected that it was here that la Rinascita, later called the Renaissance by the French, produced so many classical works of art. At that time, the city

---

1. Pope John Paul II, *The Lord and Giver of Life* (Washington, D.C.: United States Catholic Conference, 1986), 103–4.

was steeped in its Christian heritage. Looking out on the church of Santa Croce, I would try to imagine what it must have been like in those day when the Franciscan friars would fill the piazza with thousands of Florentines to hear the Good News preached. I also became intrigued as I visited churches, each with its own history and treasures of art, and wondered how all this came into being. What was the church like in those days? It was certainly alive, and people were actively involved in its life.

One day I was talking to a young Italian who described the church as he saw it today: "The church is just old buildings and old priests!" When I left him, I noted all the tourists entering and leaving the churches, looking at all their various works of art—from the past! But if you travel in Europe, you will find that in many countries the church, for whatever reason, has lost its relevancy to the young and the old. An Italian priest once told me that only about 8 percent of those who profess to be Catholic actually practice their faith.

In one parish I visited, the pastor was faced with an empty church and very few participants when he arrived. The church was built in the fourteenth century, an artistic gem, and yet he decided to move out of that building which represented the past. He built a cinder block structure a short distance from the beautiful fourteenth-century church, and the only word to describe it was ugly! And yet, on Sundays it was packed with both young and old. It was a thriving, worshipping community, and you got caught up in their lively faith. The priest was relevant and was among people who responded to him. His feeling was that the beautiful fourteenth-century church was not theirs; it belonged to another era. We need simple buildings for our churches today, he explained, and went on to say it was perhaps time for the church to give away these gems of architecture, containing great works of art and other treasures from the past, and get on with the work at hand—building new communities of worship. He said it was important not to burden this new generation with places of worship that no longer reflect them or their faith.

For centuries, the church has been the custodian of great works of art. Perhaps it had to be. But now might be the time to recognize that secular institutions can preserve these great treasures. Churches have become, in the words of one Roman priest, "museums, with caretakers who happen to be priests and religious." Now might well be the opportune moment in history to let go of these museums and initiate a new Renaissance.

When I sat in the top of the "hermitage," I often found myself dreaming of a new, reborn church. Like in the early centuries, the emphasis would be on community, formation. Once again the church would be a "school of love and friendship." The priest would be responsible for fostering the growth of the individual members and the community as a whole in the life of love, friendship, prayer, dialogue, and discipline. Above all, it would be his job to open his people to the wonders of God's love and mercy. In my dream I saw an emphasis on people rather than on buildings and structures—an emphasis on love and friendship rather than on doctrine or laws.

However, dreams are a long way from reality. Wherever I went, I found a church that seemed determined to close its ears to the hearts of the people in the streets. Surely, they must be trying to tell us something about our ministry. Why is it that the Good News that has been given to us to preach and proclaim to the world in every era is irrelevant today? Is it irrelevant, or are we the ones who have become irrelevant? Is the problem perhaps that we no longer make sense to people on their journeys?

My greatest shock came in Ireland, the land of my ancestral roots. Here too, one can't escape the fact that young people are finding that the church has no meaningful place at the center of their lives. While I was there I was talking to one young man who said that the church only made sense when the priest was "real" and preached in a way that helped him to live life and follow Christ. He said that whenever he found such a priest, he would go to mass not only on Sundays, but often during the week. But if the priest didn't make sense, he rarely went to church. On another occasion, a mother told me that she could no longer fight with her older children about going to mass on Sunday. She said that she had tried her best to raise them in the Catholic faith, and now all she could do was to pray for them. She went on to share with me that for her generation it was faith that mattered, but for the younger generation the church had to become more relevant and meaningful with regard to their daily lives. The same could be said of any place in the world today; if the priest is truly alive, if he communicates the Good News of Jesus Christ and is a builder of community, then people respond.

On May 22, 1986, with the publication of the "Vatican Report on Sects, Cults and New Religious Movements," I discovered that my thoughts in the hermitage in Florence were not just pipe dreams, but that in fact the church was indeed listening. This document speaks compellingly to the modern world of the need for authentic, meaningful change in the church. In outlining reasons for the proliferation of alternative religious movements in our day, it explains the spiritual hunger which has led so many Catholics to lose interest in the church. These reasons were listed in the Introduction, but to refresh your memory, they are:

1. Quest for Belonging (sense of community)
2. Search for Answers
3. Search for Wholeness (Holism)
4. Search for Cultural Identity
5. Need to Be Recognized
6. Search for Transcendence
7. Need of Spiritual Guidance
8. Need of Vision
9. Need of Participation and Involvement

The document goes on to suggest pastoral approaches, and points out that if they are carried out, the challenge of the sects will prove to have been a useful stimulus for spiritual and ecclesial renewal. The six pastoral approaches recommended are:

1. Sense of Community

   Traditional parish–community patterns must be restruc-
   tured to become more adapted to people's life situations.
   Parishes should be communities of faith, love, and hope
   where acceptance, understanding, reconciliation are the
   norm. They should be communities of mission, prayer,
   and celebration. And they should be open to supporting
   people with special problems, the divorced, remarried,
   handicapped, and marginalized.

2. Ongoing Formation

   The document puts strong emphasis on the need for continuing education in the faith–biblical, theological, and
   ecumenical–of both the laity and the clergy. This ongoing
   process should be both informative–conferring a deeper
   understanding of our own tradition, as well as other traditions and religious groups–and formative–guiding the
   faithful towards a deeper sense of religious commitment,
   community spirit, and transcendent awareness. The
   church should be a sign of hope to people and provide reasons for that hope. At the same time, it should ask questions as well as answer them. Throughout this process,
   there should be an emphasis on the centrality of Holy
   Scripture. Finally, the mass media of communication
   should be used more effectively to these ends.

3. Personal and Holistic Approach

   People must be helped to understand that they are unique,
   that they are loved by a personal God who has created
   their particular history from birth through death to resurrection. "Old truth" should continually become for them
   "new truth" through a genuine sense of renewal. At the
   same time, they must be provided with a framework of
   thinking that will not be shaken by every "newness" that
   comes their way. Special attention must be paid to healing
   through prayers, reconciliation, and fellowship. Pastoral
   concern should not be one-dimensional; it should extend
   not only to the spiritual, but also to the physical, psychological, social, and cultural dimensions.

4. Cultural Identity

   The issue of inculturation is fundamental. It is particularly
   stressed in responses from African parishes, which reveal

feelings of estrangement from Western forms of worship and ministry which are quite irrelevant to people's cultural environment and life situation.

5. Prayer and Worship

There must be a rethinking of the traditional Saturday evening/Sunday morning liturgy, which often fails to meaningfully impact one's daily life situation. The word of God should be rediscovered as an important community-building element. "Reception" should receive as much attention as "conservation." There should be room for joyful creativity, a belief in Christian inspiration, and a greater sense of communal celebration. Here again, inculturation is a must (with due respect for the nature of the liturgy and for the demands of universality).

There is also the need for renewal in the area of preaching. Preaching is not mere theorizing, intellectualizing and moralizing, but presupposes the witness of the preacher's life. It must speak the language of the people, demands careful preparation, and, as far as possible, should be done by a team, including lay participants. Finally, preaching and community prayer should not be confined to traditional places of worship.

6. Participation and Leadership

Most respondents are aware of the growing shortage of ordained ministers and of religious men and women. This calls for stronger promotion of diversified ministry and the ongoing formation of lay leadership. More attention should be given to the role that played by lay people who, in collaboration with their pastors, can exercise true leadership, both spiritually and pastorally. Priests should not be identified as administrators and judges, but rather as brothers, guides, consolers, and men of prayer. There is too often a distance that needs to be bridged between the faithful and the bishop, even between the bishop and his priests. The ministry of bishop and priest is a ministry of unity and communion which must become visible to the faithful.

The document goes on to quote the Extraordinary Synod of 1985, saying that, "the final report of the synod notes that the world situation is changing and that the signs of the times must be analyzed continually. The church is often seen simply as an institution, perhaps because it gives too much importance to structures and not enough to drawing people to God in Christ." For this reason, the synod emphasized the need for authentic and meaningful spiritual formation.

As I reflected and prayed on all of this, I could not help but recall the beautiful and powerful words of John Paul II, announcing once again that the Holy Spirit is indeed alive in the church and in the world today. It is indeed powerfully evident that, through the Pope's encyclical on the Holy Spirit and the "Vatican Report on Sects, Cults and New Religious Movements," the Holy Spirit has placed before us the challenge and pointed the way to meeting it.

The Vatican report I just quoted from indicates that the necessary preparation for the Jubilee Year 2000 must be the implementation of these pastoral recommendations. In them, my dream for a renewed church has been given flesh. And it is my sincere hope that the vision for a new church which they outline will become a reality in our own time. Such an event would be a new Renaissance, a dynamic rebirth that would fill people with all the richness and reality of that incredible event, the incarnation!

Another aspect of my dream was that this book would evoke some small measure of the infinite richness of our Christian heritage, and serve to affirm, challenge, and give hope to people. I pray that it has done just that for you.

I'd like to conclude by returning to the title of this book, *Lift Your Sails: The Challenge of Being a Christian.* I know from my own sailing experiences that there are times when you must shorten your sails. One does encounter storms. However, I pray that you will never pull your sails down completely, but that at least you'll hoist your storm jib and let it help you to stay on course. You'll be able to ride out the storms of your life and the Spirit will never fail you. You will reach the harbor and rejoice like any good sailor who finds safety and comfort in having arrived at a mooring that is well protected and safe. It is an exciting adventure to follow the Lord, an incredible call to intimacy and friendship. I wish you well on your own journey and pray that one day we'll meet.

God bless you!

The winds of God's grace are always blowing; we need only make the effort to lift our sails.

SUGGESTED READING

Aelred of Rievaulx. *On Spiritual Friendship,* trans. Mary Eugenia Laker, S.S.N.D. Kalamazoo, Mich.: Cistercian Publications, 1977.

Buber, Martin. *I and Thou.* New York: Charles Scribner's Sons, 1958.

De Mello, Anthony. *Awareness.* New York: Doubleday, 1990.

Frankl, Viktor E. *Man's Search for Meaning.* New York: Washington Square Press, 1963.

Harris, Paul, ed. *Silence and Stillness in Every Season.* New York: Continuum, 1997.

————. *The Fire of Silence and Stillness.* New York: Continuum, 1995.

Heschel, Abraham Joshua. *Moral Grandeur and Spiritual Audacity.* New York: Noonday Press, 1996.

———— . *Quest for God: Studies in Prayer and Symbolism.* New York: Crossroad, 1993.

Johnston, William, ed. *The Cloud of Unknowing.* Garden City, N.Y.: Doubleday/Image Books, 1973.

Keating, Thomas. *Open Mind, Open Heart.* New York: Continuum, 1986.

Levine, Steven. *A Gradual Awakening.* New York: Doubleday, 1989.

Lewis, C. S. *The Four Loves.* New York: Harcourt, Brace, 1960.

Louf, Andre. *Tuning into Grace.* Kalamazoo, Mich.: Cistercian Publications, 1992.

Main, John. *The Modern Spirituality Series.* Springfield, Ill.: Templegate Books, 1995.

————. *Word into Silence.* Paulist Press, 1981.

Meninger, William. *The Loving Search for God.* New York: Continuum, 1994.

O'Donohue, John. *Anam Cara: A Book of Celtic Wisdom.* New York: Harper Collins, 1997.

Rahner, Karl. *Encounters with Silence.* New York: Newman Press, 1969.

Raub, John Jacob. *Who Told You That You Were Naked?* New York: Crossroad, 1995.

THOMAS KEATING

OPEN MIND, OPEN HEART

Written by an acknowledged modern spiritual master, the book moves beyond "discursive meditation and particular acts to the intuitive level of contemplation." Keating gives an overview of the history of contemplative prayer in the Christian tradition, and step-by-step guidance in the method of centering prayer.

158 pages

THOMAS KEATING

THE MYSTERY OF CHRIST
The Liturgy as Christian Experience

A reflection on the contemplative dimension of Christian worship. Focusing on the liturgical year, Abbot Keating shares his theological and mystical perspective on the major feasts of the annual cycle.

160 pages

THOMAS KEATING

INVITATION TO LOVE
The Way of Christian Contemplation

In this final volume of his trilogy, Abbot Keating offers a road map, as it were, for a journey that begins when centering prayer is seriously undertaken.

160 pages

THOMAS KEATING
CRISIS OF FAITH, CRISIS OF LOVE
Revised and Expanded Edition

"Under the influence of Christian mystics such as St. John of the Cross, Keating weaves a narrative account of spiritual development that will be of . . . interest to spiritual directors and seekers." —*Booklist*

140 pages

WILLIAM A. MENINGER
THE LOVING SEARCH FOR GOD
Contemplative Prayer and The Cloud of Unknowing

"Using the 14th-century spiritual classic *The Cloud of Unknowing* as both a jumping-off place and a sustained point of reference, Meninger, a Trappist monk and retreat master, does a powerful job of explaining contemplative prayer and making it approachable for any seeker. In a nurturing, practical and easy-to-understand manner, and with an obvious affection for his subject, Meninger deals with the yearning search for God through prayer and with the distractions that can impede it—unforgiveness and unforgivenness, will, distortions of imagination, memory, and intellect. The result, filled with humor and built by means of good, solid language that flows beautifully, is an excellent guide for anyone interested in deepening his or her Christian prayer life." —*Publishers Weekly*

120 pages

WILLIAM A. MENINGER

THE PROCESS OF FORGIVENESS

In this book, Father Meninger explores the complex, but most necessary facet of spiritual life: forgiveness. He shows how we can learn to make this the most simple, yet most difficult part of our spiritual practice.

112 pages

WILLIAM A. MENINGER

THE TEMPLE OF THE LORD

And Other Stories

Composed in the form of three stories which form a triptych illustrating the spiritual life, the book examines three important facets of Christian understanding: "The Temple of the Lord," "Wisdom Built a House," and "The Messiah God."

96 pages

JOHN R. AURELIO

RETURNINGS

Life-after-Death Experiences: A Christian View

"Easy to read and full of practical insight."
　　　　　　　　　　　　　　　　—Booklist

"So, very good! What a strength and consolation this will be for many people!"　　　　　　　*—Richard Rohr*

120 pages

M. BASIL PENNINGTON
ON RETREAT WITH THOMAS MERTON

Fellow Cistercian monk and intimate friend of Merton, M. Basil Pennington wrote this book at Gethsemani Abbey where he lived in the hermitage where Merton spent his last five years. He offers an intimate glimpse of Merton's day-to-day living. With original photographs by Thomas Merton.

120 pages

M. BASIL PENNINGTON
THOMAS MERTON, BROTHER MONK
The Quest for True Freedom

"This is the Merton I knew—the seeker of God, the spiritual master. Each of the previous biographies has made its own unique contribution, but none has so explored the man's life. . . . a totally engaging and thoughtful work."

—James Finley

226 pages

LEONARD J. BOWMAN
A RETREAT WITH ST. BONAVENTURE

Bowman explicates the life of the Franciscan Bonaventure (1217–1274) for modern-day applications of his teachings.

204 pages